2016

Aries

Your Personal Horoscope 2016

Aries

21st March–20th April

igloobooks

igloobooks

Published in 2015
by Igloo Books Ltd
Cottage Farm
Sywell
NN6 0BJ
www.igloobooks.com

Produced for Igloo Books by Foulsham Publishing Ltd, The Old Barrel Store, Drayman's Lane, Marlow, Bucks SL7 2FF, England

Cover images: Thinkstock / Getty

FIR003 0815
2 4 6 8 10 9 7 5 3
ISBN 978-1-78440-581-6

This is an abridged version of material originally published in Old Moore's Horoscope and Astral Diary.

Printed and manufactured in China

CONTENTS

INTRODUCTION

Your Personal Horoscopes have been specifically created to allow you to get the most from astrological patterns and the way they have a bearing on not only your zodiac sign, but nuances within it. Using the diary section of the book you can read about the influences and possibilities of each and every day of the year. It will be possible for you to see when you are likely to be cheerful and happy or those times when your nature is in retreat and you will be more circumspect. The diary will help to give you a feel for the specific 'cycles' of astrology and the way they can subtly change your day-to-day life. For example, when you see the sign ☿, this means that the planet Mercury is retrograde at that time. Retrograde means it appears to be running backwards through the zodiac. Such a happening has a significant effect on communication skills, but this is only one small aspect of how the Personal Horoscope can help you.

With Your Personal Horoscope the story doesn't end with the diary pages. It includes simple ways for you to work out which zodiac sign was occupied by the Moon at the time of your birth, and what this means for your personality. In addition, if you know the time of day you were born, it is possible to discover your Ascendant, yet another important guide to your personal make-up and potential.

Many readers are interested in relationships and in knowing how well they get on with people of other astrological signs. You might also be interested in the way you appear to other people. If you are such a person, the section on Venus will be of particular interest. Despite the rapidly changing position of this planet, you can work out your Venus sign, and learn what bearing it will have on your life.

Using Your Personal Horoscope, you can travel on one of the most fascinating and rewarding journeys that anyone can take – the journey to a better realisation of self.

THE ESSENCE OF ARIES

Exploring the Personality of Aries the Ram

(21ST MARCH–20TH APRIL)

What's in a sign?

Aries is not the first sign of the zodiac by accident. It's the place in the year when the spring begins, and so it represents some of the most dynamic forces in nature, and within the zodiac as a whole. As a result the very essence of your nature is geared towards promoting yourself in life and pushing your ideas forward very positively. You don't brook a great deal of interference in your life, but you are quite willing to help others as much as you can, provided that to do so doesn't curb your natural desire to get on in life.

Aries people are not universally liked, though your true friends remain loyal to you under almost any circumstances. But why should it be that such a dynamic and go-getting person meets with some opposition? The answer is simple: not everyone is quite so sure of themselves as you are and many tend to get nervous when faced with the sheer power of the Aries personality. If there is one factor within your own control that could counter these problems it is the adoption of some humility – that commodity which is so important for you to dredge from the depths of your nature. If you only show the world that you are human, and that you are well aware of the fact, most people would follow you willingly to the very gates of hell. The most successful Aries subjects know this fact and cultivate it to the full.

Your executive skills are never in doubt and you can get almost anything practical done whilst others are still jumping from foot to foot. That's why you are such a good organiser and are so likely to be out there at the front of any venture. Adventurous and quite willing to show your bravery in public, you can even surprise yourself sometimes with the limits you are likely to go to in order to reach solutions that seem right to you.

Kind to those you take to, you can be universally loved when working at your best. Despite this there will be times in your life when you simply can't understand why some people just don't like you. Maybe there's an element of jealousy involved.

Aries resources

The part of the zodiac occupied by the sign of Aries has, for many centuries, been recognised as the home of self-awareness. This means that there isn't a person anywhere else in the zodiac that has a better knowledge of self than you do. But this isn't necessarily an intellectual process with Aries, more a response to the very blood that is coursing through your veins. Aries' success doesn't so much come from spending hours working out the pros and cons of any given course of action, more from the thrill of actually getting stuck in. If you find yourself forced into a life that means constantly having to think everything through to the tiniest detail, there is likely to be some frustration in evidence.

Aries is ruled by Mars, arguably the most go-getting of all the planets in the solar system. Mars is martial and demands practical ways of expressing latent power. It also requires absolute obedience from subordinates. When this is forthcoming, Aries individuals are the most magnanimous people to be found anywhere. Loyalty is not a problem and there have been many instances in history when Aries people were quite willing to die for their friends if necessary.

When other people are willing to give up and go with the flow, you will still be out there pitching for the result that seems most advantageous to you. It isn't something you can particularly control and those who don't know you well could find you sometimes curt and over-demanding as a result. But because you are tenacious you can pick the bones out of any situation and will usually arrive at your desired destination, if you don't collapse with fatigue on the way.

Routines, or having to take life at the pace of less motivated types, won't suit you at all. Imprisonment of any sort, even in a failed relationship, is sheer torture and you will move heaven and earth to get out into the big, wide world, where you can exploit your natural potential to the full. Few people know you really well because you don't always explain yourself adequately. The ones who do adore you.

Beneath the surface

Whereas some zodiac signs are likely to spend a great deal of their lives looking carefully at the innermost recesses of their own minds, Aries individuals tend to prefer the cut and thrust of the practical world. Aries people are not natural philosophers, but that doesn't mean that you aren't just as complicated beneath the surface as any of your astrological brothers and sisters. So what is it that makes the Aries firebrand think and act in the way that it does? To a great extent it is a lack of basic self-confidence.

This statement might seem rather odd, bearing in mind that a fair percentage of the people running our world were born under the sign of the Ram, but it is true nevertheless. Why? Because people who know themselves and their capabilities really well don't feel the constant need to prove themselves in the way that is the driving force of your zodiac sign. Not that your naturally progressive tendencies are a fault. On the contrary, if used correctly they can help you to create a much better, fairer and happier world, at least in your own vicinity.

The fact that you occasionally take your ball and go home if you can't get your own way is really down to the same insecurity that is noticeable through many facets of your nature. If Aries can't rule, it often doesn't want to play at all. A deep resentment and a brooding quality can build up in the minds and souls of some thwarted Aries types, a tendency that you need to combat. Better by far to try and compromise, itself a word that doesn't exist in the vocabularies of the least enlightened people born under the sign of the Ram. Once this lesson is learned, inner happiness increases and you relax into your life much more.

The way you think about others is directly related to the way you consider they think about you. This leads to another surprising fact regarding the zodiac sign. Aries people absolutely hate to be disliked, though they would move heaven and earth to prove that this isn't the case. And as a result Aries both loves and hates with a passion. Deep inside you can sometimes be a child shivering in the dark. If you only realise this fact your path to happiness and success is almost assured. Of course to do so takes a good deal of courage – but that's a commodity you don't lack.

Making the best of yourself

It would be quite clear to any observer that you are not the sort of person who likes to hang around at the back of a queue, or who would relish constantly taking orders from people who may not know situations as well as you do. For that reason alone you are better in positions that see you out there at the front, giving commands and enjoying the cut and thrust of everyday life. In a career sense this means that whatever you do you are happiest telling those around you how to do it too. Many Aries people quite naturally find their way to the top of the tree and don't usually have too much trouble staying there.

It is important to remember, however, that there is another side to your nature: the giving qualities beneath your natural dominance. You can always be around when people need you the most, encouraging and even gently pushing when it is necessary. By keeping friends and being willing to nurture relationships across a broad spectrum, you gradually get to know what makes those around you tick. This makes for a more patient and understanding sort of Aries subject – the most potent of all.

Even your resilience is not endless, which is why it is important to remember that there are times when you need rest. Bearing in mind that you are not superhuman is the hardest lesson to learn, but the admission brings humility, something that Aries needs to cultivate whenever possible.

Try to avoid living a restricted life and make your social contacts frequent and important. Realise that there is much more to life than work and spend some of your free time genuinely attempting to help those who are less well off than you are. Crucially you must remember that 'help' is not the same as domination.

The impressions you give

This section may well be of less interest to Aries subjects than it would be to certain other zodiac signs. The reason is quite clear. Aries people are far less interested in what others think about them than almost anyone else – or at least they tell themselves that they are. Either way it is counterproductive to ignore the opinions of the world at large because to do so creates stumbling blocks, even in a practical sense.

Those around you probably find you extremely capable and well able to deal with almost any situation that comes your way. Most are willing to rely heavily on you and the majority would almost instinctively see you as a leader. Whether or not they like you at the same time is really dependent on the way you handle situations. That's the difference between the go-getting, sometimes selfish type of Aries subject and the more enlightened amongst this illustrious sign.

You are viewed as being exciting and well able to raise enthusiasm for almost any project that takes your fancy. Of course this implies a great responsibility because you are always expected to come up with the goods. The world tends to put certain people on a pedestal, and you are one of them. On the other side of the coin we are all inclined to fire arrows at the elevated, so maintaining your position isn't very easy.

Most of the time you are seen as being magnanimous and kind, factors that you can exploit, whilst at the same time recognising the depth of the responsibility that comes with being an Aries subject. It might not be a bad thing to allow those around you to see that you too have feet of clay. This will make them respect and support you all the more, and even Aries people really do need to feel loved. A well-balanced Aries subject is one of the most elevated spirits to be found anywhere.

The way forward

You certainly enjoy life more when looking at it from the top of the tree. Struggling to get by is not in the least interesting to your zodiac sign and you can soon become miserable if things are not going well for you. That's why it is probably quite justified in your case to work tenaciously in order to achieve your objectives. Ideally, once you have realised some sort of success and security for yourself, you should then be willing to sit and watch life go by a little more. In fact this doesn't happen. The reason for this is clear. The Aries subject who learns how to succeed rarely knows when to stop – it's as simple as that.

Splitting your life into different components can help, if only because this means that you don't get the various elements mixed up. So, for example, don't confuse your love life with your professional needs, or your family with colleagues. This process allows you to view life in manageable chunks and also makes it possible for you to realise when any one of them may be working well. As a result you will put the effort where it's needed, and enjoy what is going well for you.

If you want to know real happiness you will also have to learn that acquisition for its own sake brings hollow rewards at best. When your talents are being turned outward to the world at large, you are one of the most potent and successful people around. What is more you should find yourself to be a much happier person when you are lending a hand to the wider world. This is possible, maybe outside of your normal professional sphere, though even where voluntary work is concerned it is important not to push yourself to the point of fatigue.

Keep yourself physically fit, without necessarily expecting that you can run to the South Pole and back, and stay away from too many stimulants, such as alcohol and nicotine. The fact is that you are best when living a healthy life, but it doesn't help either if you make even abstinence into an art form. Balance is important, as is moderation – itself a word that is difficult for you to understand. In terms of your approach to other people it's important to realise that everyone has a specific point of view. These might be different to yours, but they are not necessarily wrong. Sort out the friends who are most important to you and stick with them, whilst at the same time realising that almost everyone can be a pal – with just a little effort.

ARIES ON THE CUSP

Astrological profiles are altered for those people born at either the beginning or the end of a zodiac sign, or, more properly, on the cusps of a sign. In the case of Aries this would be on the 21st of March and for two or three days after, and similarly at the end of the sign, probably from the 18th to the 20th of April.

The Pisces Cusp – March 21st to March 24th

With the Sun so close to the zodiac sign of Pisces at the time you were born, it is distinctly possible that you have always had some doubts when reading a character breakdown written specifically for the sign of Aries. This isn't surprising because no zodiac sign has a definite start or end, they merely merge together. As a result there are some of the characteristics of the sign of the Fishes that are intermingled with the qualities of Aries in your nature.

What we probably find, as a result, is a greater degree of emotional sensitivity and a tendency to be more cognisant of what the rest of humanity is feeling. This is not to imply that Aries is unfeeling, but rather that Pisceans actively make humanity their business.

You are still able to achieve your most desired objectives in the practical world, but on the way, you stop to listen to the heartbeat of the planet on which you live. A very good thing, of course, but at the same time there is some conflict created if your slightly dream-like tendencies get in the way of your absolute need to see things through to their logical conclusion.

Nobody knows you better than you know yourself, or at least that's what the Aries qualities within you say, but that isn't always verified by some of the self-doubt that comes from the direction of the Fishes. As in all matters astrological, a position of balance has to be achieved in order to reconcile the differing qualities of your nature. In your case, this is best accomplished by being willing to stop and think once in a while and by refusing to allow your depth to be a problem.

Dealt with properly, the conjoining of Pisces and Aries can be a wondrous and joyful affair, a harmony of opposites that always makes you interesting to know. Your position in the world is naturally one of authority but at the same time you need to serve. That's why some people with this sort of mixture of astrological qualities would make such good administrators in a hospital, or in any position where the alternate astrological needs are well balanced. In the chocolate box of life you are certainly a 'soft centre'.

The Taurus Cusp – April 18th to April 20th

The merge from Aries to Taurus is much less well defined than the one at the other side of Aries, but it can be very useful to you all the same. Like the Pisces-influenced Aries you may be slightly more quiet than would be the case with the Ram taken alone and your thought processes are probably not quite as fast. But to compensate for this fact you don't rush into things quite as much and are willing to allow ideas to mature more fully.

Your sense of harmony and beauty is strong and you know, in a very definite way, exactly what you want. As a result your home will be distinctive but tasteful and it's a place where you need space to be alone sometimes, which the true Aries subject probably does not. You do not lack the confidence to make things look the way you want them, but you have a need to display these things to the world at large and sometimes even to talk about how good you are at decoration and design.

If anyone finds you pushy, it is probably because they don't really know what makes you tick. Although you are willing to mix with almost anyone, you are more inclined, at base, to have a few very close friends who stay at the forefront of your life for a long time. It is likely that you enjoy refined company and you wouldn't take kindly to the dark, the sordid, or the downright crude in life.

Things don't get you down as much as can sometimes be seen to be the case for Taurus when taken alone and you are rarely stumped for a progressive and practical idea when one is needed most. At all levels, your creative energy is evident and some of you even have the ability to make this into a business, since Aries offers the practical and administrative spark that Taurus can sometimes lack.

In matters of love, you are ardent and sincere, probably an idealist, and you know what you want in a partner. Whilst this is also true in the case of Taurus, you are different, because you are much more likely, not only to look, but also to say something about the way you feel.

Being naturally friendly you rarely go short of the right sort of help and support when it is most vital. Part of the reason for this lies in the fact that you are so willing to be the sounding-board for the concerns of your friends. All in all you can be very contented with your lot, but you never stop searching for something better all the same. At its best, this is one of the most progressive cuspal matches of them all.

ARIES AND ITS ASCENDANTS

The nature of every individual on the planet is composed of the rich variety of zodiac signs and planetary positions that were present at the time of their birth. Your Sun sign, which in your case is Aries, is one of the many factors when it comes to assessing the unique person you are. Probably the most important consideration, other than your Sun sign, is to establish the zodiac sign that was rising over the eastern horizon at the time that you were born. This is your Ascending or Rising sign. Most popular astrology fails to take account of the Ascendant, and yet its importance remains with you from the very moment of your birth, through every day of your life. The Ascendant is evident in the way you approach the world, and so, when meeting a person for the first time, it is this astrological influence that you are most likely to notice first. Our Ascending sign essentially represents what we appear to be, while our Sun sign is what we feel inside ourselves.

The Ascendant also has the potential for modifying our overall nature. For example, if you were born at a time of day when Aries was passing over the eastern horizon (this would be around the time of dawn) then you would be classed as a double Aries. As such you would typify this zodiac sign, both internally and in your dealings with others. However, if your Ascendant sign turned out to be a Water sign, such as Pisces, there would be a profound alteration of nature, away from the expected qualities of Aries.

One of the reasons that popular astrology often ignores the Ascendant is that it has always been rather difficult to establish. We have found a way to make this possible by devising an easy-to-use table, which you will find on page 157 of this book. Using this, you can establish your Ascendant sign at a glance. You will need to know your rough time of birth, then it is simply a case of following the instructions.

For those readers who have no idea of their time of birth it might be worth allowing a good friend, or perhaps your partner, to read through the section that follows this introduction. Someone who deals with you on a regular basis may easily discover your Ascending sign, even though you could have some difficulty establishing it for yourself. A good understanding of this component of your nature is essential if you want to be aware of that 'other person' who is responsible for the way you make contact with the world at large. Your Sun sign, Ascendant sign, and the other pointers in this book

will, together, allow you a far better understanding of what makes you tick as an individual. Peeling back the different layers of your astrological make-up can be an enlightening experience, and the Ascendant may represent one of the most important layers of all.

Aries with Aries Ascendant

What you see is what you get with this combination. You typify the no-nonsense approach of Aries at its best. All the same this combination is quite daunting when viewed through the eyes of other, less dominant sorts of people. You tend to push your way though situations that would find others cowering in a corner and you are afraid of very little. With a determination to succeed that makes you a force to be reckoned with, you leave the world in no doubt as to your intentions and tend to be rather too brusque for your own good on occasions.

At heart you are kind and loving, able to offer assistance to the downtrodden and sad, and usually willing to take on board the cares of people who have a part to play in your life. No-one would doubt your sincerity, or your honesty, though you may utilise slightly less than orthodox ways of getting your own way on those occasions when you feel you have right on your side. You are a loving partner and a good parent, though where children are concerned you tend to be rather too protective. The trouble is that you know what a big, bad world it can be and probably feel that you are better equipped to deal with things than anyone else.

Aries with Taurus Ascendant

This is a much quieter combination, so much so that even experienced astrologers would be unlikely to recognise you as an Aries subject at all, unless of course they came to know you very well. Your approach to life tends to be quiet and considered and there is a great danger that you could suppress those feelings that others of your kind would be only too willing to verbalise. To compensate you are deeply creative and will think matters through much more readily than more dominant Aries types would be inclined to do. Reaching out towards the world, you are, nevertheless, somewhat locked inside yourself and can struggle to achieve the level of communication that you so desperately need. Frustration might easily follow, were it not for the fact that you possess a quiet determination that, to those in the know, is the clearest window through to your Aries soul.

The care for others is stronger here than with almost any other Aries type and you certainly demonstrate this at all levels. The fact is that you live a great percentage of your life in service to the people you take to, whilst at the same time being able to shut the door firmly in the face of people who irritate or anger you. You are deeply motivated towards family relationships.

Aries with Gemini Ascendant

A fairly jolly combination this, though by no means easy for others to come to terms with. You fly about from pillar to post and rarely stop long enough to take a breath. Admittedly this suits your own needs very well, but it can be a source of some disquiet to those around you, since they may not possess your energy or motivation. Those who know you well are deeply in awe of your capacity to keep going long after almost everyone else would have given up and gone home, though this quality is not always as wonderful as it sounds because it means that you put more pressure on your nervous system than just about any other astrological combination.

You need to be mindful of your nervous system, which responds to the erratic, mercurial quality of Gemini. Problems only really arise when the Aries part of you makes demands that the Gemini component finds difficult to deal with. There are paradoxes galore here and some of them need sorting out if you are ever fully to understand yourself, or are to be in a position when others know what makes you tick.

In relationships you might be a little fickle, but you are a real charmer and never stuck for the right words, no matter who you are dealing with. Your tenacity knows no bounds, though perhaps it should!

Aries with Cancer Ascendant

The main problem that you experience in life shows itself as a direct result of the meshing of these two very different zodiac signs. At heart Aries needs to dominate, whereas Cancer shows a desire to nurture. All too often the result can be a protective arm that is so strong that nobody could possibly get out from under it. Lighten your own load, and that of those you care for, by being willing to sit back and watch others please themselves a little. You might think that you know best, and your heart is clearly in the right place, but try to realise what life is like when someone is always on hand to tell you that they know better then you do.

But in a way this is a little severe, because you are fairly intuitive and your instincts would rarely lead you astray. Nobody could ask for a better partner or parent than you, though they might request a slightly less attentive one. In matters of work you are conscientious and are probably best suited to a job that means sorting out the kind of mess that humanity is so good at creating. You probably spend your spare time untangling balls of wool, though you are quite sporting too and could easily make the Olympics. Once there you would not win however, because you would be too concerned about all the other competitors.

Aries with Leo Ascendant

Here we come upon the first situation of Aries being allied with another Fire sign. This creates a character that could appear to be typically Aries at first sight and in many ways it is, though there are subtle differences that should not be ignored. Although you have the typical Aries ability to get things done, many of the tasks you do undertake will be for and on behalf of others. You can be proud, and on some occasions even haughty, and yet you are also regal in your bearing and honest to the point of absurdity. Nobody could doubt your sincerity and you have the soul of a poet combined with the courage of a lion.

All this is good, but it makes you rather difficult to approach, unless the person in question has first adopted a crouching and subservient attitude although you would not wish them to do so. It's simply that the impression you give and the motivation that underpins it are two quite different things. You are greatly respected and in the case of those individuals who know your real nature, you are also deeply loved. But life would be much simpler if you didn't always have to fight the wars that those around you are happy to start. Relaxation is a word that you don't really understand and you would do yourself a favour if you looked it up in a dictionary.

Aries with Virgo Ascendant

Virgo is steady and sure, though also fussy and stubborn. Aries is fast and determined, restless and active. It can already be seen that this is a rather strange meeting of characteristics and because Virgo is ruled by the capricious Mercury, the ultimate result will change from hour to hour and day to day. It isn't merely that others find it difficult to know where they are with you, they can't even understand what makes you tick. This will make you the subject of endless fascination and attention, at which you will be apparently surprised but inwardly pleased. If anyone ever really gets to know what goes on in that busy mind they may find the implications very difficult to deal with and it is a fact that only you would have the ability to live inside your crowded head.

As a partner and a parent you are second to none, though you tend to get on better with your children once they start to grow, since by this time you may be slightly less restricting to their own desires, which will often clash with your own on their behalf. You are capable of give and take and could certainly not be considered selfish, though your constant desire to get the best from everyone might occasionally be misconstrued.

Aries with Libra Ascendant

Libra has the tendency to bring out the best in any zodiac sign, and this is no exception when it comes together with Aries. You may, in fact, be the most comfortable of all Aries types, simply because Libra tempers some of your more assertive qualities and gives you the chance to balance out opposing forces, both inside yourself and in the world outside. You are fun to be with and make the staunchest friend possible. Although you are generally affable, few people would try to put one over on you, because they would quickly come to know how far you are willing to go before you let forth a string of invective that would shock those who previously underestimated your basic Aries traits.

Home and family are very dear to you, but you are more tolerant than some Aries types are inclined to be and you have a youthful zest for life that should stay with you no matter what age you manage to achieve. There is always something interesting to do and your mind is a constant stream of possibilities. This makes you very creative and you may also demonstrate a desire to look good at all times. You may not always be quite as confident as you appear to be, but few would guess the fact.

Aries with Scorpio Ascendant

The two very different faces of Mars come together in this potent, magnetic and quite awe-inspiring combination. Your natural inclination is towards secrecy and this fact, together with the natural attractions of the sensual Scorpio nature, makes you the object of great curiosity. This means that you will not go short of attention and should ensure that you are always being analysed by people who may never get to know you at all. At heart you prefer your own company, and yet life appears to find means to push you into the public gaze time and again. Most people with this combination ooze sex appeal and can use this fact as a stepping stone to personal success, yet without losing any integrity or loosening the cords of a deeply moralistic nature.

On those occasions when you do lose your temper, there isn't a character in the length and breadth of the zodiac who would have either the words or the courage to stand against the stream of invective that follows. On really rare occasions you might even scare yourself. As far as family members are concerned a simple look should be enough to show when you are not amused. Few people are left unmoved by your presence in their life.

Aries with Sagittarius Ascendant

What a lovely combination this can be, for the devil-may-care aspects of Sagittarius lighten the load of a sometimes too-serious Aries interior. Everything that glistens is not gold, though it's hard to convince you of the fact because, to mix metaphors, you can make a silk purse out of a sow's ear. Almost everyone loves you and in return you offer a friendship that is warm and protective, but not as demanding as sometimes tends to be the case with the Aries type. Relationships may be many and varied and there is often more than one major attachment in the life of those holding this combination. You will bring a breath of spring to any attachment, though you need to ensure that the person concerned is capable of keeping up with the hectic pace of your life.

It may appear from time to time that you are rather too trusting for your own good, though deep inside you are very astute and it seems that almost everything you undertake works out well in the end. This has nothing to do with native luck and is really down to the fact that you are much more calculating than might appear to be the case at first sight. As a parent you are protective yet offer sufficient room for self-expression.

Aries with Capricorn Ascendant

If ever anyone could be accused of setting off immediately, but slowly, it has to be you. These are very contradictory signs and the differences will express themselves in a variety of ways. One thing is certain, you have tremendous tenacity and will see a job through patiently from beginning to end, without tiring on the way, and ensuring that every detail is taken care of properly. This combination often bestows good health and a great capacity for continuity, particularly in terms of the length of life. You are certainly not as argumentative as the typical Aries, but you do know how to get your own way, which is just as well because you are usually thinking on behalf of everyone else and not just on your own account.

At home you can relax, which is a blessing for Aries, though in fact you seldom choose to do so because you always have some project or other on the go. You probably enjoy knocking down and rebuilding walls, though this is a practical tendency and not responsive to relationships, in which you are ardent and sincere. Impetuosity is as close to your heart as is the case for any type of Aries subject, though you certainly have the ability to appear patient and steady. But it's just a front, isn't it?

Aries with Aquarius Ascendant

The person standing on a soap box in the corner of the park, extolling the virtues of this or that, could quite easily be an Aries with an Aquarian Ascendant. You are certainly not averse to speaking your mind and you have plenty to talk about because you are the best social reformer and political animal of them all. Unorthodox in your approach, you have the ability to keep everyone guessing, except when it comes to getting your own way, for in this nobody doubts your natural abilities. You can put theories into practice very well and on the way you retain a sense of individuality that would shock more conservative types. It's true that a few people might find you a little difficult to approach and this is partly because you have an inner reserve and strength which is difficult for others to fathom.

In the world at large you take your place at the front, as any good Arian should, and yet you offer room for others to share your platform. You keep up with the latest innovations and treat family members as the genuine friends that you believe them to be. Care needs to be taken when picking a life partner, for you are an original, and not just anyone could match the peculiarities thrown up by this astrological combination.

Aries with Pisces Ascendant

Although not an easy combination to deal with, the Aries with a Piscean Ascendant does, nevertheless, bring something very special to the world in the way of natural understanding allied to practical assistance. It's true that you can sometimes be a dreamer, but there is nothing wrong with that as long as you have the ability to turn some of your wishes into reality, and this you are easily able to do, usually for the sake of those around you. Conversation comes easily to you, though you also possess a slightly wistful and poetic side to your nature, which is attractive to the many people who call you a friend. A natural entertainer, you bring a sense of the comic to the often serious qualities of Aries, though without losing the determination that typifies the sign.

In relationships you are ardent, sincere and supportive, with a strong social conscience that sometimes finds you fighting the battles of the less privileged members of society. Family is important to you and this is a combination that invariably leads to parenthood. Away from the cut and thrust of everyday life you relax more fully and think about matters more deeply than more typical Aries types might.

THE MOON AND THE PART IT PLAYS IN YOUR LIFE

In astrology the Moon is probably the single most important heavenly body after the Sun. Its unique position, as partner to the Earth on its journey around the solar system, means that the Moon appears to pass through the signs of the zodiac extremely quickly. The zodiac position of the Moon at the time of your birth plays a great part in personal character and is especially significant in the build-up of your emotional nature.

Your Own Moon Sign

Discovering the position of the Moon at the time of your birth has always been notoriously difficult because tracking the complex zodiac positions of the Moon is not easy. This process has been reduced to three simple stages with our Lunar Tables. A breakdown of the Moon's zodiac positions can be found from page 35 onwards, so that once you know what your Moon Sign is, you can see what part this plays in the overall build-up of your personal character.

If you follow the instructions on the next page you will soon be able to work out exactly what zodiac sign the Moon occupied on the day that you were born and you can then go on to compare the reading for this position with those of your Sun sign and your Ascendant. It is partly the comparison between these three important positions that goes towards making you the unique individual you are.

HOW TO DISCOVER YOUR MOON SIGN

This is a three-stage process. You may need a pen and a piece of paper but if you follow the instructions below the process should only take a minute or so.

STAGE 1 First of all you need to know the Moon Age at the time of your birth. If you look at Moon Table 1, on page 33, you will find all the years between 1918 and 2016 down the left side. Find the year of your birth and then trace across to the right to the month of your birth. Where the two intersect you will find a number. This is the date of the New Moon in the month that you were born. You now need to count forward the number of days between the New Moon and your own birthday. For example, if the New Moon in the month of your birth was shown as being the 6th and you were born on the 20th, your Moon Age Day would be 14. If the New Moon in the month of your birth came after your birthday, you need to count forward from the New Moon in the previous month. If you were born in a Leap Year, remember to count the 29th February. You can tell if your birth year was a Leap Year if the last two digits can be divided by four. Whatever the result, jot this number down so that you do not forget it.

STAGE 2 Take a look at Moon Table 2 on page 34. Down the left hand column look for the date of your birth. Now trace across to the month of your birth. Where the two meet you will find a letter. Copy this letter down alongside your Moon Age Day.

STAGE 3 Moon Table 3 on page 34 will supply you with the zodiac sign the Moon occupied on the day of your birth. Look for your Moon Age Day down the left hand column and then for the letter you found in Stage 2. Where the two converge you will find a zodiac sign and this is the sign occupied by the Moon on the day that you were born.

Your Zodiac Moon Sign Explained

You will find a profile of all zodiac Moon Signs on pages 35 to 38, showing in yet another way how astrology helps to make you into the individual that you are. In each daily entry of the Astral Diary you can find the zodiac position of the Moon for every day of the year. This also allows you to discover your lunar birthdays. Since the Moon passes through all the signs of the zodiac in about a month, you can expect something like twelve lunar birthdays each year. At these times you are likely to be emotionally steady and able to make the sort of decisions that have real, lasting value.

MOON TABLE 1

YEAR	FEB	MAR	APR	YEAR	FEB	MAR	APR	YEAR	FEB	MAR	APR
1918	11	12	11	1951	6	7	6	1984	1	2	1
1919	–	2/31	30	1952	25	25	24	1985	19	21	20
1920	19	20	18	1953	14	15	13	1986	9	10	9
1921	8	9	8	1954	3	5	3	1987	28	29	28
1922	26	28	27	1955	22	24	22	1988	17	18	16
1923	15	17	16	1956	11	12	11	1989	6	7	6
1924	5	5	4	1957	–	1/31	29	1990	25	26	25
1925	23	24	23	1958	18	20	19	1991	14	15	13
1926	12	14	12	1959	7	9	8	1992	3	4	3
1927	2	3	2	1960	26	27	26	1993	22	24	22
1928	19	21	20	1961	15	16	15	1994	10	12	11
1929	9	11	9	1962	5	6	5	1995	29	30	29
1930	28	30	28	1963	23	25	23	1996	18	19	18
1931	17	19	18	1964	13	14	12	1997	7	9	7
1932	6	7	6	1965	1	2	1	1998	26	27	26
1933	24	26	24	1966	19	21	20	1999	16	17	16
1934	14	15	13	1967	9	10	9	2000	5	6	4
1935	3	5	3	1968	28	29	28	2001	23	24	23
1936	22	23	21	1969	17	18	16	2002	12	13	12
1937	11	13	12	1970	6	7	6	2003	–	2	1
1938	–	2/31	30	1971	25	26	25	2004	20	21	19
1939	19	20	19	1972	14	15	13	2005	9	10	8
1940	8	9	7	1973	4	5	3	2006	28	29	27
1941	26	27	26	1974	22	24	22	2007	15	18	17
1942	15	16	15	1975	11	12	11	2008	6	7	6
1943	4	6	4	1976	29	30	29	2009	25	26	25
1944	24	24	22	1977	18	19	18	2010	14	15	14
1945	12	14	12	1978	7	9	7	2011	3	5	3
1946	2	3	2	1979	26	27	26	2012	22	22	21
1947	19	21	20	1980	15	16	15	2013	10	12	10
1948	9	11	9	1981	4	6	4	2014	1	1/31	30
1949	27	29	28	1982	23	24	23	2015	19	20	19
1950	16	18	17	1983	13	14	13	2016	8	8	7

TABLE 2

DAY	MAR	APR
1	F	J
2	G	J
3	G	J
4	G	J
5	G	J
6	G	J
7	G	J
8	G	J
9	G	J
10	G	J
11	G	K
12	H	K
13	H	K
14	H	K
15	H	K
16	H	K
17	H	K
18	H	K
19	H	K
20	H	K
21	H	L
22	I	L
23	I	L
24	I	L
25	I	L
26	I	L
27	I	L
28	I	L
29	I	L
30	I	L
31	I	–

MOON TABLE 3

M/D	F	G	H	I	J	K	L
0	PI	PI	AR	AR	AR	TA	TA
1	PI	AR	AR	AR	TA	TA	TA
2	AR	AR	AR	TA	TA	TA	GE
3	AR	AR	TA	TA	TA	GE	GE
4	AR	TA	TA	GE	GE	GE	GE
5	TA	TA	GE	GE	GE	CA	CA
6	TA	GE	GE	GE	CA	CA	CA
7	GE	GE	GE	CA	CA	CA	LE
8	GE	GE	CA	CA	CA	LE	LE
9	CA	CA	CA	CA	LE	LE	VI
10	CA	CA	LE	LE	LE	VI	VI
11	CA	LE	LE	LE	VI	VI	VI
12	LE	LE	LE	VI	VI	VI	LI
13	LE	LE	VI	VI	VI	LI	LI
14	VI	VI	VI	LI	LI	LI	LI
15	VI	VI	LI	LI	LI	SC	SC
16	VI	LI	LI	LI	SC	SC	SC
17	LI	LI	LI	SC	SC	SC	SA
18	LI	LI	SC	SC	SC	SA	SA
19	LI	SC	SC	SC	SA	SA	SA
20	SC	SC	SA	SA	SA	CP	CP
21	SC	SA	SA	SA	CP	CP	CP
22	SC	SA	SA	CP	CP	CP	AQ
23	SA	SA	CP	CP	CP	AQ	AQ
24	SA	CP	CP	CP	AQ	AQ	AQ
25	CP	CP	AQ	AQ	AQ	PI	PI
26	CP	AQ	AQ	AQ	PI	PI	PI
27	AQ	AQ	AQ	PI	PI	PI	AR
28	AQ	AQ	PI	PI	PI	AR	AR
29	AQ	PI	PI	PI	AR	AR	AR

AR = Aries, TA = Taurus, GE = Gemini, CA = Cancer, LE = Leo, VI = Virgo, LI = Libra, SC = Scorpio, SA = Sagittarius, CP = Capricorn, AQ = Aquarius, PI = Pisces

MOON SIGNS

Moon in Aries

You have a strong imagination, courage, determination and a desire to do things in your own way and forge your own path through life.

Originality is a key attribute; you are seldom stuck for ideas although your mind is changeable and you could take the time to focus on individual tasks. Often quick-tempered, you take orders from few people and live life at a fast pace. Avoid health problems by taking regular time out for rest and relaxation.

Emotionally, it is important that you talk to those you are closest to and work out your true feelings. Once you discover that people are there to help, there is less necessity for you to do everything yourself.

Moon in Taurus

The Moon in Taurus gives you a courteous and friendly manner, which means you are likely to have many friends.

The good things in life mean a lot to you, as Taurus is an Earth sign that delights in experiences which please the senses. Hence you are probably a lover of good food and drink, which may in turn mean you need to keep an eye on the bathroom scales, especially as looking good is also important to you.

Emotionally you are fairly stable and you stick by your own standards. Taureans do not respond well to change. Intuition also plays an important part in your life.

Moon in Gemini

You have a warm-hearted character, sympathetic and eager to help others. At times reserved, you can also be articulate and chatty: this is part of the paradox of Gemini, which always brings duplicity to the nature. You are interested in current affairs, have a good intellect, and are good company and likely to have many friends. Most of your friends have a high opinion of you and would be ready to defend you should the need arise. However, this is usually unnecessary, as you are quite capable of defending yourself in any verbal confrontation.

Travel is important to your inquisitive mind and you find intellectual stimulus in mixing with people from different cultures. You also gain much from reading, writing and the arts but you do need plenty of rest and relaxation in order to avoid fatigue.

Moon in Cancer

The Moon in Cancer at the time of birth is a fortunate position as Cancer is the Moon's natural home. This means that the qualities of compassion and understanding given by the Moon are especially enhanced in your nature, and you are friendly and sociable and cope well with emotional pressures. You cherish home and family life, and happily do the domestic tasks. Your surroundings are important to you and you hate squalor and filth. You are likely to have a love of music and poetry.

Your basic character, although at times changeable like the Moon itself, depends on symmetry. You aim to make your surroundings comfortable and harmonious, for yourself and those close to you.

Moon in Leo

The best qualities of the Moon and Leo come together to make you warm-hearted, fair, ambitious and self-confident. With good organisational abilities, you invariably rise to a position of responsibility in your chosen career. This is fortunate as you don't enjoy being an 'also-ran' and would rather be an important part of a small organisation than a menial in a large one.

You should be lucky in love, and happy, provided you put in the effort to make a comfortable home for yourself and those close to you. It is likely that you will have a love of pleasure, sport, music and literature. Life brings you many rewards, most of them as a direct result of your own efforts, although you may be luckier than average and ready to make the best of any situation.

Moon in Virgo

You are endowed with good mental abilities and a keen receptive memory, but you are never ostentatious or pretentious. Naturally quite reserved, you still have many friends. Marital relationships must be discussed carefully and worked at so that they remain harmonious, as personal attachments can be a problem if you do not give them your full attention.

Talented and persevering, you possess artistic qualities and are a good homemaker. Earning your honours through genuine merit, you work long and hard towards your objectives but show little pride in your achievements. Many short journeys will be undertaken in your life.

Moon in Libra

With the Moon in Libra you are naturally popular and make friends easily. People like you, probably more than you realise, you bring fun to a party and are a natural diplomat. For all its good points, Libra is not the most stable of astrological signs and, as a result, your emotions can be a little unstable too. Therefore, although the Moon in Libra is said to be good for love and marriage, your Sun sign and Rising sign will have an important effect on your emotional and loving qualities.

You must remember to relate to others in your decision-making. Co-operation is crucial because Libra represents the 'balance' of life that can only be achieved through harmonious relationships. Conformity is not easy for you because Libra, an Air sign, likes its independence.

Moon in Scorpio

Some people might call you pushy. In fact, all you really want to do is to live life to the full and protect yourself and your family from the pressures of life. Take care to avoid giving the impression of being sarcastic or impulsive and use your energies wisely and constructively.

You have great courage and you invariably achieve your goals by force of personality and sheer effort. You are fond of mystery and are good at predicting the outcome of situations and events. Travel experiences can be beneficial to you.

You may experience problems if you do not take time to examine your motives in a relationship, and also if you allow jealousy, always a feature of Scorpio, to cloud your judgement.

Moon in Sagittarius

The Moon in Sagittarius helps to make you a generous individual with humanitarian qualities and a kind heart. Restlessness may be intrinsic as your mind is seldom still. Perhaps because of this, you have a need for change that could lead you to several major moves during your adult life. You are not afraid to stand your ground when you know your judgement is right, you speak directly and have good intuition.

At work you are quick, efficient and versatile and so you make an ideal employee. You need work to be intellectually demanding and do not enjoy tedious routines.

In relationships, you anger quickly if faced with stupidity or deception, though you are just as quick to forgive and forget. Emotionally, there are times when your heart rules your head.

Moon in Capricorn

The Moon in Capricorn makes you popular and likely to come into the public eye in some way. The watery Moon is not entirely comfortable in the Earth sign of Capricorn and this may lead to some difficulties in the early years of life. An initial lack of creative ability and indecision must be overcome before the true qualities of patience and perseverance inherent in Capricorn can show through.

You have good administrative ability and are a capable worker, and if you are careful you can accumulate wealth. But you must be cautious and take professional advice in partnerships, as you are open to deception. You may be interested in social or welfare work, which suit your organisational skills and sympathy for others.

Moon in Aquarius

The Moon in Aquarius makes you an active and agreeable person with a friendly, easy-going nature. Sympathetic to the needs of others, you flourish in a laid-back atmosphere. You are broad-minded, fair and open to suggestion, although sometimes you have an unconventional quality which others can find hard to understand.

You are interested in the strange and curious, and in old articles and places. You enjoy trips to these places and gain much from them. Political, scientific and educational work interests you and you might choose a career in science or technology.

Money-wise, you make gains through innovation and concentration and Lunar Aquarians often tackle more than one job at a time. In love you are kind and honest.

Moon in Pisces

You have a kind, sympathetic nature, somewhat retiring at times, but you always take account of others' feelings and help when you can.

Personal relationships may be problematic, but as life goes on you can learn from your experiences and develop a better understanding of yourself and the world around you.

You have a fondness for travel, appreciate beauty and harmony and hate disorder and strife. You may be fond of literature and would make a good writer or speaker yourself. You have a creative imagination and may come across as an incurable romantic. You have strong intuition, maybe bordering on a mediumistic quality, which sets you apart from the mass. You may not be rich in cash terms, but your personal gifts are worth more than gold.

ARIES IN LOVE

Discover how compatible in love you are with people from the same and other signs of the zodiac. Five stars equals a match made in heaven!

Aries meets Aries

This could be an all-or-nothing pairing. Both parties are from a dominant sign, so someone will have to be flexible in order to maintain personal harmony. Both know what they want out of life, and may have trouble overcoming any obstacles a relationship creates. This is a good physical pairing, with a chemistry that few other matches enjoy to the same level. Attitude is everything, but at least there is a mutual admiration that makes gazing at your partner like looking in the mirror. Star rating: ****

Aries meets Taurus

This is a match that has been known to work very well. Aries brings dynamism and ambition, while Taurus has the patience to see things through logically. Such complementary views work equally well in a relationship or in the office. There is mutual respect, but sometimes a lack of total understanding. The romantic needs of each are quite different, but both are still fulfilled. They can live easily in domestic harmony which is very important but, interestingly, Aries may be the loser in battles of will. Star rating: ***

Aries meets Gemini

Don't expect peace and harmony with this combination, although what comes along instead might make up for any disagreements. Gemini has a very fertile imagination, while Aries has the tenacity to make reality from fantasy. Combined, they have a sizzling relationship. There are times when both parties could explode with indignation and something has to give. But even if there are clashes, making them up will always be most enjoyable! Mutual financial success is likely in this match. Star rating: ****

Aries meets Cancer

A potentially one-sided pairing, it often appears that the Cancerian is brow-beaten by the far more dominant Arian. So much depends on the patience of the Cancerian individual, because if good psychology is present – who knows? But beware, Aries, you may find your partner too passive, and constantly having to take the lead can be wearing – even for you. A prolonged trial period would be advantageous, as the match could easily go either way. When it does work, though, this relationship is usually contented. Star rating: ***

Aries meets Leo

Stand by for action and make sure the house is sound-proof. Leo is a lofty idealist and there is always likely to be friction when two Fire signs meet. To compensate, there is much mutual admiration, together with a desire to please. Where there are shared incentives, the prognosis is good but it's important not to let little irritations blow up. Both signs want to have their own way and this is a sure cause of trouble. There might not be much patience here, but there is plenty of action. Star rating: *****

Aries meets Virgo

Neither of these signs really understands the other, and that could easily lead to a clash. Virgo is so pedantic, which will drive Aries up the wall, while Aries always wants to be moving on to the next objective, before Virgo is even settled with the last one. It will take time for these two to get to know each other, but this is a great business matching. If a personal relationship is seen in these terms then the prognosis can be good, but on the whole, this is not an inspiring match. Star rating: ***

Aries meets Libra

These signs are zodiac opposites which means a make-or-break situation. The match will either be a great success or a dismal failure. Why? Well Aries finds it difficult to understand the flighty Air-sign tendencies of Libra, whilst the natural balance of Libra contradicts the unorthodox Arian methods. Any flexibility will come from Libra, which may mean that things work out for a while, but Libra only has so much patience and it may eventually run out. In the end, Aries may be just too bossy for an independent but sensitive sign like Libra. Star rating: **

Aries meets Scorpio

There can be great affection here, even if the two zodiac signs are so very different. The common link is the planet Mars, which plays a part in both these natures. Although Aries is, outwardly, the most dominant, Scorpio people are among the most powerful to be found anywhere. This quiet determination is respected by Aries. Aries will satisfy the passionate side of Scorpio, particularly with instruction from Scorpio. There are mysteries here which will add spice to life. The few arguments that do occur are likely to be awe-inspiring. Star rating: ****

Aries meets Sagittarius

This can be one of the most favourable matches of them all. Both Aries and Sagittarius are Fire signs, which often leads to clashes of will, but this pair find a mutual understanding. Sagittarius helps Aries to develop a better sense of humour, while Aries teaches the Archer about consistency on the road to success. Some patience is called for on both sides, but these people have a natural liking for each other. Add this to growing love and you have a long-lasting combination that is hard to beat. Star rating: *****

Aries meets Capricorn

Capricorn works conscientiously to achieve its objectives and so can be the perfect companion for Aries. The Ram knows how to achieve but not how to consolidate, so the two signs have a great deal to offer one another practically. There may not be fireworks and it's sometimes doubtful how well they know each other, but it may not matter. Aries is outwardly hot but inwardly cool, whilst Capricorn can appear low key but be a furnace underneath. Such a pairing can gradually find contentment, though both parties may wonder how this is so. Star rating: ****

Aries meets Aquarius

Aquarius is an Air sign, and Air and Fire often work well together, but perhaps not in the case of Aries and Aquarius. The average Aquarian lives in what the Ram sees as a fantasy world, so without a sufficiently good meeting of minds, compromise may be lacking. Of course, almost anything is possible, and the dominant side of Aries could be trained by the devil-may-care attitude of Aquarius. There are meeting points but they are difficult to establish. However, given sufficient time and an open mind on both sides, a degree of happiness is possible. Star rating: **

Aries meets Pisces

Still waters run deep, and they don't come much deeper than Pisces. Although these signs share the same quadrant of the zodiac, they have little in common. Pisces is a dreamer, a romantic idealist with steady and spiritual goals. Aries needs to be on the move, and has very different ideals. It's hard to see how a relationship could develop because the outlook on life is so different but, with patience, especially from Aries, there is a chance that things might work out. Pisces needs incentive, and Aries may be the sign to offer it. Star rating: **

VENUS: THE PLANET OF LOVE

If you look up at the sky around sunset or sunrise you will often see Venus in close attendance to the Sun. It is arguably one of the most beautiful sights of all and there is little wonder that historically it became associated with the goddess of love. But although Venus does play an important part in the way you view love and in the way others see you romantically, this is only one of the spheres of influence that it enjoys in your overall character.

Venus has a part to play in the more cultured side of your life and has much to do with your appreciation of art, literature, music and general creativity. Even the way you look is responsive to the part of the zodiac that Venus occupied at the start of your life, though this fact is also down to your Sun sign and Ascending sign. If, at the time you were born, Venus occupied one of the more gregarious zodiac signs, you will be more likely to wear your heart on your sleeve, as well as to be more attracted to entertainment, social gatherings and good company. If on the other hand Venus occupied a quiet zodiac sign at the time of your birth, you would tend to be more retiring and less willing to shine in public situations.

It's good to know what part the planet Venus plays in your life for it can have a great bearing on the way you appear to the rest of the world and since we all have to mix with others, you can learn to make the very best of what Venus has to offer you.

One of the great complications in the past has always been trying to establish exactly what zodiac position Venus enjoyed when you were born because the planet is notoriously difficult to track. However, we have solved that problem by creating a table that is exclusive to your Sun sign, which you will find on the following page.

Establishing your Venus sign could not be easier. Just look up the year of your birth on the following page and you will see a sign of the zodiac. This was the sign that Venus occupied in the period covered by your sign in that year. If Venus occupied more than one sign during the period, this is indicated by the date on which the sign changed, and the name of the new sign. For instance, if you were born in 1950, Venus was in Aquarius until the 7th April, after which time it was in Pisces. If you were born before 7th April your Venus sign is Aquarius, if you were born on or after 7th April, your Venus sign is Pisces. Once you have established the position of Venus at the time of your birth, you can then look in the pages which follow to see how this has a bearing on your life as a whole.

1918 AQUARIUS / 5.4 PISCES
1919 ARIES / 24.3 TAURUS
1920 PISCES / 14.4 ARIES
1921 TAURUS
1922 ARIES / 13.4 TAURUS
1923 AQUARIUS / 1.4 PISCES
1924 TAURUS / 6.4 GEMINI
1925 PISCES / 28.3 ARIES
1926 AQUARIUS / 6.4 PISCES
1927 ARIES / 24.3 TAURUS
1928 PISCES / 13.4 ARIES
1929 TAURUS / 20.4 ARIES
1930 ARIES / 13.4 TAURUS
1931 AQUARIUS / 31.3 PISCES
1932 TAURUS / 6.4 GEMINI
1933 PISCES / 27.3 ARIES
1934 AQUARIUS / 6.4 PISCES
1935 ARIES / 23.3 TAURUS
1936 PISCES / 13.4 ARIES
1937 TAURUS / 14.4 ARIES
1938 ARIES / 12.4 TAURUS
1939 AQUARIUS / 31.3 PISCES
1940 TAURUS / 5.4 GEMINI
1941 PISCES / 26.3 ARIES / 20.4 TAURUS
1942 AQUARIUS / 7.4 PISCES
1943 ARIES / 23.3 TAURUS
1944 PISCES / 12.4 ARIES
1945 TAURUS / 8.4 ARIES
1946 ARIES / 12.4 TAURUS
1947 AQUARIUS / 30.3 PISCES
1948 TAURUS / 5.4 GEMINI
1949 PISCES / 25.3 ARIES / 20.4 TAURUS
1950 AQUARIUS / 7.4 PISCES
1951 ARIES / 22.3 TAURUS
1952 PISCES / 12.4 ARIES
1953 TAURUS / 1.4 ARIES
1954 ARIES / 11.4 TAURUS
1955 AQUARIUS / 30.3 PISCES
1956 TAURUS / 4.4 GEMINI
1957 PISCES / 25.3 ARIES / 19.4 TAURUS
1958 AQUARIUS / 8.4 PISCES
1959 ARIES / 22.3 TAURUS
1960 PISCES / 11.4 ARIES
1961 ARIES
1962 ARIES / 11.4 TAURUS
1963 AQUARIUS / 29.3 PISCES
1964 TAURUS / 4.4 GEMINI
1965 PISCES / 24.3 ARIES / 19.4 TAURUS
1966 AQUARIUS / 8.4 PISCES
1967 TAURUS / 20.4 GEMINI
1968 PISCES / 10.4 ARIES
1969 ARIES
1970 ARIES / 10.4 TAURUS
1971 AQUARIUS / 29.3 PISCES
1972 TAURUS / 3.4 GEMINI
1973 PISCES / 24.3 ARIES / 18.4 TAURUS
1974 AQUARIUS / 8.4 PISCES
1975 TAURUS / 19.4 GEMINI
1976 PISCES / 10.4 ARIES
1977 ARIES
1978 ARIES / 10.4 TAURUS
1979 AQUARIUS / 28.3 PISCES
1980 TAURUS / 3.4 GEMINI
1981 PISCES / 23.3 ARIES / 18.4 TAURUS
1982 AQUARIUS / 9.4 PISCES
1983 TAURUS / 19.4 GEMINI
1984 PISCES / 9.4 ARIES
1985 ARIES
1986 ARIES / 9.4 TAURUS
1987 AQUARIUS / 28.3 PISCES
1988 TAURUS / 2.4 GEMINI
1989 PISCES / 23.3 ARIES / 17.4 TAURUS
1990 AQUARIUS / 9.4 PISCES
1991 TAURUS / 18.4 GEMINI
1992 PISCES / 9.4 ARIES
1993 ARIES
1994 ARIES / 9.4 TAURUS
1995 AQUARIUS / 27.3 PISCES
1996 TAURUS / 2.4 GEMINI
1997 PISCES / 22.3 ARIES / 17.4 TAURUS
1998 AQUARIUS / 9.4 PISCES
1999 TAURUS / 18.4 GEMINI
2000 PISCES / 9.4 ARIES
2001 ARIES
2002 ARIES / 7.4 TAURUS
2003 AQUARIUS / 27.3 PISCES
2004 TAURUS / 1.4 GEMINI
2005 PISCES/22.3 ARIES
2006 AQUARIUS/7.4 PISCES
2007 TAURUS / 16.4 GEMINI
2008 PISCES / 9.4 ARIES
2009 ARIES
2010 ARIES / 7.4 TAURUS
2011 AQUARIUS / 27.3 PISCES
2012 TAURUS / 1.4 GEMINI
2013 PISCES / 22.3 ARIES
2014 AQUARIUS / 7.4 PISCES
2015 TAURUS / 16.4 GEMINI
2016 PISCES / 9.4 ARIES

VENUS THROUGH THE ZODIAC SIGNS

Venus in Aries

Amongst other things, the position of Venus in Aries indicates a fondness for travel, music and all creative pursuits. Your nature tends to be affectionate and you would try not to create confusion or difficulty for others if it could be avoided. Many people with this planetary position have a great love of the theatre, and mental stimulation is of the greatest importance. Early romantic attachments are common with Venus in Aries, so it is very important to establish a genuine sense of romantic continuity. Early marriage is not recommended, especially if it is based on sympathy. You may give your heart a little too readily on occasions.

Venus in Taurus

You are capable of very deep feelings and your emotions tend to last for a very long time. This makes you a trusting partner and lover, whose constancy is second to none. In life you are precise and careful and always try to do things the right way. Although this means an ordered life, which you are comfortable with, it can also lead you to be rather too fussy for your own good. Despite your pleasant nature, you are very fixed in your opinions and quite able to speak your mind. Others are attracted to you and historical astrologers always quoted this position of Venus as being very fortunate in terms of marriage. However, if you find yourself involved in a failed relationship, it could take you a long time to trust again.

Venus in Gemini

As with all associations related to Gemini, you tend to be quite versatile, anxious for change and intelligent in your dealings with the world at large. You may gain money from more than one source but you are equally good at spending it. There is an inference here that you are a good communicator, via either the written or the spoken word, and you love to be in the company of interesting people. Always on the look-out for culture, you may also be very fond of music, and love to indulge the curious and cultured side of your nature. In romance you tend to have more than one relationship and could find yourself associated with someone who has previously been a friend or even a distant relative.

Venus in Cancer

You often stay close to home because you are very fond of family and enjoy many of your most treasured moments when you are with those you love. Being naturally sympathetic, you will always do anything you can to support those around you, even people you hardly know at all. This charitable side of your nature is your most noticeable trait and is one of the reasons why others are naturally so fond of you. Being receptive and in some cases even psychic, you can see through to the soul of most of those with whom you come into contact. You may not commence too many romantic attachments but when you do give your heart, it tends to be unconditionally.

Venus in Leo

It must become quickly obvious to almost anyone you meet that you are kind, sympathetic and yet determined enough to stand up for anyone or anything that is truly important to you. Bright and sunny, you warm the world with your natural enthusiasm and would rarely do anything to hurt those around you, or at least not intentionally. In romance you are ardent and sincere, though some may find your style just a little overpowering. Gains come through your contacts with other people and this could be especially true with regard to romance, for love and money often come hand in hand for those who were born with Venus in Leo. People claim to understand you, though you are more complex than you seem.

Venus in Virgo

Your nature could well be fairly quiet no matter what your Sun sign might be, though this fact often manifests itself as an inner peace and would not prevent you from being basically sociable. Some delays and even the odd disappointment in love cannot be ruled out with this planetary position, though it's a fact that you will usually find the happiness you look for in the end. Catapulting yourself into romantic entanglements that you know to be rather ill-advised is not sensible, and it would be better to wait before you committed yourself exclusively to any one person. It is the essence of your nature to serve the world at large and through doing so it is possible that you will attract money at some stage in your life.

Venus in Libra

Venus is very comfortable in Libra and bestows upon those people who have this planetary position a particular sort of kindness that is easy to recognise. This is a very good position for all sorts of friendships and also for romantic attachments that usually bring much joy into your life. Few individuals with Venus in Libra would avoid marriage and since you are capable of great depths of love, it is likely that you will find a contented personal life. You like to mix with people of integrity and intelligence but don't take kindly to scruffy surroundings or work that means getting your hands too dirty. Careful speculation, good business dealings and money through marriage all seem fairly likely.

Venus in Scorpio

You are quite open and tend to spend money quite freely, even on those occasions when you don't have very much. Although your intentions are always good, there are times when you get yourself in to the odd scrape and this can be particularly true when it comes to romance, which you may come to late or from a rather unexpected direction. Certainly you have the power to be happy and to make others contented on the way, but you find the odd stumbling block on your journey through life and it could seem that you have to work harder than those around you. As a result of this, you gain a much deeper understanding of the true value of personal happiness than many people ever do, and are likely to achieve true contentment in the end.

Venus in Sagittarius

You are lighthearted, cheerful and always able to see the funny side of any situation. These facts enhance your popularity. You should never have to look too far to find romantic interest in your life, though it is just possible that you might be too willing to commit yourself before you are certain that the person in question is right for you. Part of the problem here extends to other areas of life too. The fact is that you like variety in everything and so can tire of situations that fail to offer it. All the same, if you choose wisely and learn to understand your restless side, then great happiness can be yours.

Venus in Capricorn

The most notable trait that comes from Venus in this position is that it makes you trustworthy and able to take on all sorts of responsibilities in life. People are instinctively fond of you and love you all the more because you are always ready to help those who are in any form of need. Social and business popularity can be yours and there is a magnetic quality to your nature that is particularly attractive in a romantic sense. Anyone who wants a partner for a lover, a spouse and a good friend too would almost certainly look in your direction. Constancy is the hallmark of your nature and unfaithfulness would go right against the grain. You might sometimes be a little too trusting.

Venus in Aquarius

This location of Venus offers a fondness for travel and a desire to try out something new at every possible opportunity. You are extremely easy to get along with and tend to have many friends from varied backgrounds, classes and inclinations. You like to live a distinct sort of life and gain a great deal from moving about, both in a career sense and with regard to your home. It is not out of the question that you could form a romantic attachment to someone who comes from far away or be attracted to a person of a distinctly artistic and original nature. What you cannot stand is jealousy, for you have friends of both sexes and would want to keep things that way.

Venus in Pisces

The first thing people tend to notice about you is your wonderful, warm smile. Being very charitable by nature you will do anything to help others, even if you don't know them well. Much of your life may be spent sorting out situations for other people, but it is very important to feel that you are living for yourself too. In the main, you remain cheerful, and tend to be quite attractive to other people. Where romantic attachments are concerned, you could be drawn to people who are significantly older or younger than yourself or to someone with a unique career or point of view. It might be best for you to avoid marrying whilst you are still very young.

ARIES: 2015 DIARY PAGES

October

2015

1 THURSDAY ☿ *Moon Age Day 18 Moon Sign Taurus*

There could be a few troublesome domestic issues to be sorted out at this stage of the week and that might mean getting behind in other matters. Exercise all the patience you can and simply do what seems most necessary. You can catch up later and in any case it comes down to being a matter of priorities in the end.

2 FRIDAY ☿ *Moon Age Day 19 Moon Sign Gemini*

Communication issues could run into difficulty if you don't keep on top of them. The basic reason is that others will misunderstand what you are trying to tell them and it is therefore very important that you double-check that messages are coming across as you intend. This is more likely to be an issue at work than in social settings.

3 SATURDAY ☿ *Moon Age Day 20 Moon Sign Gemini*

A good deal of adapting will be necessary at the moment if you want to get the very best out of life. For the last few days you have been under the influence of a few slightly awkward planetary influences and these could have left you feeling somewhat muddled. Today offers you the chance to think things through and to take action.

4 SUNDAY ☿ *Moon Age Day 21 Moon Sign Gemini*

Don't be bossy at home and allow family members to choose options for themselves. You don't mean to interfere, it's just your way, but others may not be all that happy about the fact that you seem to know better than they do how to run their lives. If you listen and comment but avoid interference you can still have an input.

5 MONDAY ☿ *Moon Age Day 22 Moon Sign Cancer*

This could be one of the best times of the month for involving yourself in community issues and for getting to grips with a slight problem that has a bearing on just about everyone you know. You are very socially minded at the moment and the reforming tendencies of Aries show out strongly. You might even be quite political.

6 TUESDAY ☿ *Moon Age Day 23 Moon Sign Cancer*

Don't allow the views of others to influence your judgements to such an extent that you fail to address issues yourself. Aries might be just a little lazy at the moment and for that reason alone it will be easier to simply go with the flow. Force yourself to think about matters yourself and take whatever actions your mind suggests.

7 WEDNESDAY ☿ *Moon Age Day 24 Moon Sign Leo*

Your sensitivity is heightened and it looks as though you will be doing a great deal to support others today. There ought to be more time to address issues that are associated with your home life and family members will be pleased to have you around more. Your sunny and warm personality can be a joy to almost everyone you meet.

8 THURSDAY ☿ *Moon Age Day 25 Moon Sign Leo*

You enjoy a good balance of give and take right now and should find certain individuals to be far more giving than might have been the case only a few days ago. With plenty of determination you won't be easily beaten but there might be one particular issue that despite all your efforts should now be reluctantly abandoned.

9 FRIDAY ☿ *Moon Age Day 26 Moon Sign Virgo*

Organisational issues take up a good deal of your time at the moment. This could be related to work but is just as likely to be concerned with social issues and your need to ring the changes in terms of out-of-work interests. Keep in touch with friends who are at a distance and maybe arrange a long journey to be taken next year.

10 SATURDAY ☿ *Moon Age Day 27 Moon Sign Virgo*

Don't allow yourself to be manipulated by others. Rather, you need to look at all situations yourself and to react according to your own conscience. Aries is a natural leader and not a follower, which is why in the end you can bring others round to your own point of view. It's a fine line though because bullying won't work.

11 SUNDAY ☿ *Moon Age Day 28 Moon Sign Virgo*

A restless streak starts to become evident and ordinary, everyday tasks could be something you will run a mile to avoid. You need a change of scenery and even if you only manage to get an hour or two in your local park it could be enough to make you feel entirely different. Learn to delegate and let others do some of the work.

12 MONDAY *Moon Age Day 29 Moon Sign Libra*

The Moon is now firmly in your opposite zodiac sign and is almost certain to bring stumbling blocks that you will have to work hard to get through or round. It might actually be better not to try too hard, but rather to wait for better trends before committing yourself to anything that requires real effort.

13 TUESDAY *Moon Age Day 0 Moon Sign Libra*

If you struggle to stay on top of things today, you have to ask yourself whether it is even necessary in some cases. There might be certain issues that would be best left to their own devices, whilst you concentrate of matters that are self-evidently important. In any case, your capabilities are going to be much improved tomorrow.

14 WEDNESDAY *Moon Age Day 1 Moon Sign Scorpio*

This is a good day for constructive career building and for planning ahead as far as your professional life is concerned. There could be a slight lull in romantic potential, but that is probably because you are so busy doing other things. Try not to be too selective about jobs and sort out some of the less pleasant ones, too.

15 THURSDAY *Moon Age Day 2 Moon Sign Scorpio*

The social contacts you have been making of late can be of great use to you right now. This will be especially true in professional situations. Don't be too surprised if you are being sought out for special treatment from those in authority and show how pleased you are when someone close to home seeks your opinion, too.

16 FRIDAY *Moon Age Day 3 Moon Sign Scorpio*

If there have been specific worries at the back of your mind, you should discover that at least a few of them now disappear like the morning mist. Maybe you have worried them out of existence, but it is far more likely that you were making too much of an issue of them in the first place. A feeling of significant relief could follow.

17 SATURDAY *Moon Age Day 4 Moon Sign Sagittarius*

The support you now receive from others should be stronger at the moment than has seemed to be the case for quite some time. Make use of this situation by relying on colleagues and good friends, whilst at the same time checking details and making certain that you are still fully in command of all situations yourself.

18 SUNDAY *Moon Age Day 5 Moon Sign Sagittarius*

This is an excellent time to be on the move and the chances of you making some real gains in the material world are extremely good. At the same time, you should remember that this is a Sunday. The year is moving on rapidly towards its end and the weather will hardly be improving. Get some fresh air and enjoy the great outdoors while you can.

19 MONDAY *Moon Age Day 6 Moon Sign Capricorn*

Stand by for a busier time in store, though not particularly for today. Plan ahead, but without pushing yourself too much at the start of this working week. For most Aries people, it will be enough to say what you want in order for others to do their best to see your plans mature. You have some good friends around you now.

20 TUESDAY *Moon Age Day 7 Moon Sign Capricorn*

There is a great deal in your chart now about self-expression, leisure and pleasure. All you need in order to make today go with a real swing is a good dose of optimism, together with the support of like-minded friends. Personal attachments should be strengthening and family members actively seek your advice around now.

21 WEDNESDAY *Moon Age Day 8 Moon Sign Capricorn*

It is important to take life one step at a time and to avoid being overwhelmed if everything seems to be happening at once. Don't bite off more than you can chew at work and when you are at home allow relatives or your partner to do something on your behalf. This isn't the most energetic day of the month for you.

22 THURSDAY *Moon Age Day 9 Moon Sign Aquarius*

Now you begin to show real insight and your independent approach to life is both refreshing and useful. Not everyone seems to have your best interests at heart, but you do have what it takes to turn situations to your advantage, no matter what others might think. You should be dreaming up new and revolutionary ways to do tedious jobs.

23 FRIDAY *Moon Age Day 10 Moon Sign Aquarius*

Emotional confrontations are to be strictly avoided today. There is a distinct possibility that you could get yourself involved in some sort of argument that will be both pointless and potentially destructive. When it comes to issues about which you have no real opinion, make it plain that you are willing to be flexible.

24 SATURDAY *Moon Age Day 11 Moon Sign Pisces*

Social pleasure can now be integrated into your overall plans for the weekend. This is a good time to mix business with pleasure and to get satisfaction from both. You may begin new friendships at this time and also get a positive response from people who are in positions of authority. All in all, a positive period for Aries.

25 SUNDAY *Moon Age Day 12 Moon Sign Pisces*

A few delays are more or less inevitable at the moment and there appears to be little you can do about the situation but wait and see. That might leave you with time on your hands. Since you can easily get restless, right now you need to take on new projects that give your active mind something to think about.

26 MONDAY *Moon Age Day 13 Moon Sign Aries*

Stand by for an explosion of possibilities and do everything you can to meet this very progressive period in a reactive way. The 'lunar high' should bring better general luck, together with a fund of new incentives and plenty of energy to pursue them. All in all this could be the most influential day that you will encounter during October.

27 TUESDAY *Moon Age Day 14 Moon Sign Aries*

This is the best time of the month to be running ahead of the pack. So quick are your thought processes that it is unlikely many people will be able to keep up with you. The new incentives continue and at the same time you have what it takes to sweep someone right off their feet. As a result new romance is possible for some.

28 WEDNESDAY *Moon Age Day 15 Moon Sign Taurus*

Things continue in a very positive way and some situations seem to be turning to your advantage, even without you trying very hard. A combination of past effort and present certainties allows you to glide towards your objectives, whilst on the surface you appear to be the coolest and most collected person around.

29 THURSDAY *Moon Age Day 16 Moon Sign Taurus*

There could be internal relationship matters causing some slight anxiety around now, but this is not created by a powerful or long-lasting astrological trend. For most of the time you are easy-going and find that those with whom you mix during the day are just as relaxed as you are. This could be a good day to ask for a favour.

30 FRIDAY *Moon Age Day 17 Moon Sign Gemini*

You should press on with your daily business, generally unconcerned about issues that are not really yours to sort out. If you get yourself tied down with worries that rightfully belong to other people, you will slow your own progress. It's fine to stand up for your friends, but don't try to live their lives for them.

31 SATURDAY *Moon Age Day 18 Moon Sign Gemini*

It isn't what happens on the surface that really interests you today, but rather the undercurrents of life. For once Aries becomes a deep thinker and your intuition is turned up full. You can do yourself a great deal of good, both personally and professionally, by tuning in to what people are thinking rather than what they are saying.

November

2015

1 SUNDAY *Moon Age Day 19 Moon Sign Cancer*

Today should be good for all matters that involve communication with others. Not only do you know what to say, but you also have a good idea about the best way to approach different sorts of people. Some routine tasks should be passed to others right now, whilst you deal with the most important jobs.

2 MONDAY *Moon Age Day 20 Moon Sign Cancer*

A romantic matter might give you the run-around today, which is why you need to be paying attention and to ignore any sort of goading that appears to be taking place. Stick to what you know and stay cool when provocation is around. You have the patience to win the day easily if you simply take your time.

3 TUESDAY *Moon Age Day 21 Moon Sign Leo*

Intimate encounters should look good today. The closer you are to any given individual, the more willing you should be to spend time in his or her company. Dealing with strangers is likely to be far less appealing and you may prefer to stick to what you know whilst present trends continue.

4 WEDNESDAY *Moon Age Day 22 Moon Sign Leo*

In some situations it appears that others get the upper hand. As long as you play it cool this doesn't really matter. Even matters that look distinctly difficult can be dealt with smoothly if you simply choose the right words. Give yourself time to think about a necessary change of scenery that is on offer.

5 THURSDAY *Moon Age Day 23 Moon Sign Leo*

Finding the best qualities in others is often natural to you, and is an ability that is much enhanced right now. As a result you can increase your own confidence because you know you are getting the support you need. This makes it easier to take a few calculated risks that could mean significant movement in your life.

6 FRIDAY *Moon Age Day 24 Moon Sign Virgo*

There is a chance that some helpful news from faraway places could turn the tide of certain situations at the moment. Getting on with what is necessary can be something of a chore and it is quite possible that you will decide to alter your routines. Not everyone finds this easy to come to terms with, but those you really care about will co-operate.

7 SATURDAY *Moon Age Day 25 Moon Sign Virgo*

Getting on well depends not only on what you do but also on whom you know. That is certainly the case for you today. Comfort and security, whilst they have a part to play in your thinking, are not really all that important right now. You may be climbing personal mountains, and that isn't always easy.

8 SUNDAY *Moon Age Day 26 Moon Sign Libra*

Energy and enthusiasm are low and they won't get too much better for the next couple of days. Before today is out the Moon occupies the zodiac sign of Libra, bringing the 'lunar low' as far as you are concerned. Take life steadily. Enjoy a laugh in the company of friends, but avoid pushing too hard towards any destination.

9 MONDAY *Moon Age Day 27 Moon Sign Libra*

Although you are still quiet and life may not be offering what you would wish early in the day, the 'lunar low' soon passes and you can enjoy a generally happy and even eventful sort of Monday. Get the dross out of the way before lunch and then set out on a journey of self-discovery – but take a friend along.

10 TUESDAY *Moon Age Day 28 Moon Sign Libra*

A sense of general impatience permeates your life today. For a week or more now you have been trying to settle yourself, not an easy process for anyone born under your astrological sign. Little by little you are getting where you want to be, but Rome wasn't built in a day. Aries needs to be both positive and patient.

11 WEDNESDAY *Moon Age Day 29 Moon Sign Scorpio*

Relationships are now boosted by better communications and it's easier to get on with even usually awkward family members. Make the most of positive trends financially and be willing to take a small risk if necessary. Generally speaking this is not an ideal time for solo projects. Co-operation works best.

12 THURSDAY *Moon Age Day 0 Moon Sign Scorpio*

What you hear from others could be of tremendous importance today, so it is worthwhile hanging on to every snippet of gossip that comes your way. Ring the Thursday Moon Age Day changes by getting out of the house at some stage during the day. Of course, if you are committed to work that won't be a problem.

13 FRIDAY *Moon Age Day 1 Moon Sign Sagittarius*

You are likely to find yourself busy and on the go today, whether you like it or not. The chance of a stay-at-home, domestic sort of Friday is unlikely. However, once you have the bit between your teeth you will relish the cut and thrust of everyday life and can really make progress on all fronts.

14 SATURDAY *Moon Age Day 2 Moon Sign Sagittarius*

Domestic matters may find you more involved than has been possible for a week or so. Your mind turns towards the needs that loved ones have of you at present and there is plenty of reason to suspect that most of your spare time is being used to make others feel more secure. Leave a few moments just for yourself.

15 SUNDAY *Moon Age Day 3 Moon Sign Sagittarius*

It looks as though under present trends you will enjoy the company of a wide range of different sorts of people. You show great charm and a willingness to take the other person's point of view on board a little more than would sometimes be the case. If you are at work, look out for new avenues for your existing talents.

16 MONDAY *Moon Age Day 4 Moon Sign Capricorn*

Professional developments should be on a roll today and you have what it takes to make a good impression on just about everyone you meet. Don't be fooled into thinking that someone knows better than you do about any aspect of your life, because you are especially shrewd, calculating and in the know at present.

17 TUESDAY *Moon Age Day 5 Moon Sign Capricorn*

You can glean some profound insights today and show yourself to be very astute and even quite psychic. In a practical sense, you need to dump outmoded concepts or efforts that have proven themselves to be a waste of time. Don't chase rainbows that you know are going to disappear as soon as you approach them.

18 WEDNESDAY *Moon Age Day 6 Moon Sign Aquarius*

Following the same general pattern that has been obvious for a while now, you tend to break ties that are no longer of any use to you and will be making new friendships all the time. The potential for romance is good and especially so for Aries people who are presently forming new attachments or formalising more casual ones.

19 THURSDAY *Moon Age Day 7 Moon Sign Aquarius*

Your inner drive is fully in gear and what you want more than anything at the moment is to feel that you are improving in every possible way. This might lead you to a desire to remodel yourself even more, perhaps through diets or health regimes. If so you need to proceed carefully. You can achieve anything in time, but be steady.

20 FRIDAY *Moon Age Day 8 Moon Sign Pisces*

There could be an intimate issue that is on your mind at the moment and if this is the case you ought to get it sorted out before you move on to other matters. There are some small surprises in store at present and though most of these will work to your advantage you do need to be in a position to respond to situations quickly.

21 SATURDAY *Moon Age Day 9 Moon Sign Pisces*

Dream up something to do that pleases you exclusively. You've done a great deal of thinking and acting on behalf of others during the last couple of weeks and you now deserve a treat yourself. Things are going to get very hectic at the start of next week so also think about taking life steadily on this early winter Saturday.

22 SUNDAY *Moon Age Day 10 Moon Sign Aries*

A combination of factors, including the arrival of the 'lunar high', puts you firmly in the driving seat of your own life and offers great incentives when it matters the most. Consider yourself to be in the most favoured position of the month and do whatever is necessary to prove how capable you are in the eyes of others.

23 MONDAY *Moon Age Day 11 Moon Sign Aries*

The positive trends are set to continue today and you will be able to start the working week on a very positive note. Niggles from the past can be dealt with in a flash and there could be plenty of opportunities for breaking new ground. Your social instincts look especially good.

24 TUESDAY *Moon Age Day 12 Moon Sign Taurus*

There is now the same powerful desire to get things done that typifies your zodiac sign. The restrictions are out of the way and nothing will hold you back when you are certain of the direction you wish to take. Pay attention to what your partner or a good friend is saying. If you do, you could save yourself a lot of effort.

25 WEDNESDAY *Moon Age Day 13 Moon Sign Taurus*

A desire for personal freedom is now so strong within you that you would do almost anything to avoid feeling fettered. There is nothing at all odd about this as far as you are concerned. The fact is that Aries needs space and can soon get very frustrated and even ill if it is restricted to places or situations that feel constraining.

26 THURSDAY *Moon Age Day 14 Moon Sign Gemini*

This is a fascinating day to be out and about and it should not be spent doing either boring or routine jobs. If your time is your own find some way to get out and about, most rewardingly in the company of someone you love to be with. The evening could offer interesting social possibilities, as well as some new sort of diversion.

27 FRIDAY *Moon Age Day 15 Moon Sign Gemini*

You can apply your intuition to problem-solving today and should have a good deal of fun on the way. There are areas of your life that might need improving, or else things you want to address out there in the world as a whole. Whatever you turn your mind to at present is grist to the mill of your curiosity.

28 SATURDAY *Moon Age Day 16 Moon Sign Cancer*

This is going to be a good day when it comes to problem solving and with regard to personal advancement. Now is the time to let those in positions of authority know how good you are and today could be the focus of new responsibilities. Whatever the demands are you are up for them and should be enjoying life.

29 SUNDAY *Moon Age Day 17 Moon Sign Cancer*

You should be in for a happy phase at home and will be creating an especially caring and sharing sort of environment for yourself and your loved ones. The most pleasing moments you encounter today are likely to come along courtesy of family members and you show yourself to have more time than usual for domestic issues.

30 MONDAY *Moon Age Day 18 Moon Sign Cancer*

It looks as though career issues are going your way and there are possible gains coming in a number of different potential directions. Remove obstacles from your path when it is possible to do so, but also be willing to listen to the advice of someone who is an expert and who does know better than you.

♈

December 2015

1 TUESDAY *Moon Age Day 19 Moon Sign Leo*

This is a day of busy comings and goings. Avoid arguments and direct confrontation, unless you know it is absolutely necessary. Relatives and friends should be rather more co-operative than strangers, some of whom you may tend to mistrust. Some of your natural Aries boldness could be taking a holiday.

2 WEDNESDAY *Moon Age Day 20 Moon Sign Leo*

This is a time when you would really gain from a complete change of direction. Travel of any sort would be good and you need the cut and thrust of everyday life in order to be happy with your lot. Concern for the underdog is strong and the brave qualities of Aries are on display.

3 THURSDAY *Moon Age Day 21 Moon Sign Virgo*

This is a period to be consolidating on recent efforts. Although you might not get quite as much done in a concrete sense as you would wish you can still get ahead. Part of the secret is to allow other people to take some of the strain. This is a particularly good interlude for making contact with friends at a distance.

4 FRIDAY *Moon Age Day 22 Moon Sign Virgo*

There is now a strong emphasis on physical pleasures and on luxury. To others, you appear to be the most entertaining person around and this is a situation that is not likely to change markedly for the next few days. You can afford to push your luck and insist on getting your own way in at least a few respects.

5 SATURDAY *Moon Age Day 23 Moon Sign Libra*

It would be hard to keep ploughing on regardless in the face of the 'lunar low', but that's probably what you are going to do right now. All the encouragement in the world to rest and wait is likely to fall on deaf ears with Aries now. So if things go pear shaped and you end up fatigued, don't say you were not warned!

6 SUNDAY *Moon Age Day 24 Moon Sign Libra*

You can't expect to make quite the level of practical or professional progress you might wish, but maybe that isn't particularly important to you on a Sunday. Despite the 'lunar low', you get much from personal attachments and it is towards those you care about the most that your mind is turning at this time of year.

7 MONDAY *Moon Age Day 25 Moon Sign Libra*

It seems as if the main focus is now definitely on communication, probably with all manner of people you haven't had a great deal to do with previously. You know how to have a good time at the moment and will be quite willing to put yourself out to please others. However, it might be sensible to keep a lower profile at work.

8 TUESDAY *Moon Age Day 26 Moon Sign Scorpio*

Whilst concentration regarding detailed tasks may suffer somewhat today you can enjoy personal matters to the full. It's true that not everyone seems to be quite in line with your thinking but you can probably have some fun talking them round. There are signs that an old flame could burn again in your life any time now.

9 WEDNESDAY *Moon Age Day 27 Moon Sign Scorpio*

You may insist on being the team leader today. Although this could put someone's back up a little, it's true that you do have what it takes to head almost any faction. Avoid arguments by installing a second in command, which should keep the most contentious individuals quiet. Avoid intrigue at all cost.

10 THURSDAY *Moon Age Day 28 Moon Sign Sagittarius*

There is likely to be much to discuss today and your powers of communication are especially noteworthy at present. Strong opinions predominate around you, but it's good to know that your own considerations are being taken on board. How could they fail to be? You are an Aries, after all.

11 FRIDAY *Moon Age Day 0 Moon Sign Sagittarius*

You should be a rather good listener today and the sympathy and understanding you show for others marks you out as being very much softer by nature than you sometimes wish to appear. You will even enjoy doing the odd good turn, especially for people you think have recently had a hard time.

12 SATURDAY *Moon Age Day 1 Moon Sign Sagittarius*

You may be even more outgoing and sociable than usual at the moment. The Sun presently occupies a position that is sure to put you at the head of things. At the same time, you relish the company of many different sorts of people, most of whom find you fascinating and good to have around.

13 SUNDAY *Moon Age Day 2 Moon Sign Capricorn*

You tend to be more and more outgoing as the days slip by and will certainly be in the limelight where social situations are concerned. For some reason your popularity is especially high now. It could be that you are presently encountering many different invitations and you will be loath to turn down any of them.

14 MONDAY *Moon Age Day 3 Moon Sign Capricorn*

Today should see a boost to practical affairs that continues to work in your favour. If it seems you are somewhat short of cash, delve deep into your originality and think up new ways to earn more. The upcoming Christmas season now becomes a serious issue in your mind – somewhat belatedly, it might seem.

15 TUESDAY *Moon Age Day 4 Moon Sign Aquarius*

There is much to gain from all co-operative ventures at this time and particularly so in the case of Aries people who are involved in business partnerships. Personal attachments are also well starred. It might be the magic of the season, but you could find you feel deeply romantic and more inclined to speak words of love.

16 WEDNESDAY *Moon Age Day 5 Moon Sign Aquarius*

You now have quicker access to information that can easily be turned to your advantage. If you are involved in some inward battle, for example stopping smoking or trying to control your weight, keep up your efforts, but at the same time avoid being quite as hard on yourself as might sometimes be the case.

17 THURSDAY *Moon Age Day 6 Moon Sign Pisces*

You tend to be slightly more excitable today and could easily be overreacting to situations that would normally not move you much at all. Avoid arguing simply for the sake of doing so and whenever possible take the line of least resistance in discussions. If you shoot from the hip too much you will regret it later.

18 FRIDAY *Moon Age Day 7 Moon Sign Pisces*

With the Moon in your solar twelfth house at the moment it is clear that you become better at expressing sympathy and that your ability to see what makes others tick is more enhanced than usual. Today might be slightly quieter, but if so this is only because you are happy to watch, wait and listen for a few hours.

19 SATURDAY *Moon Age Day 8 Moon Sign Aries*

You can easily get others to see things your way, which could turn out to be one of the most gratifying aspects of this period. Confidence is growing and even if it isn't possible to address the professional or practical aspects of life today it should be clear that at least your prior planning is on course. A good day is on the cards.

20 SUNDAY *Moon Age Day 9 Moon Sign Aries*

Your thinking tends to be inspired and with the 'lunar high' present you can put many of your most important thoughts into action. It's time to get busy and to show everyone who you are and what you are capable of doing. On the way you should encounter more than your fair share of good luck.

21 MONDAY *Moon Age Day 10 Moon Sign Aries*

This could be an ideal time for travel and also for spiritual studies of almost any sort. There is something quite introspective about you right now, though this is a period that will only last for a few days. Talk to as many different sorts of people as proves to be possible today.

22 TUESDAY *Moon Age Day 11 Moon Sign Taurus*

Practical setbacks are possible and when they come along all you can do is to deal with them one at a time. By tomorrow everything should look quite different, which is why it would be sensible to shelve certain jobs until later. If you don't, you could find yourself having to repeat them later in any case.

23 WEDNESDAY *Moon Age Day 12 Moon Sign Taurus*

Although Christmas is generally a time for families and close friendships, Aries has the ability to use the social gatherings in order to further professional objectives. This could certainly be the case today, particularly since your cheerful and happy nature is making a favourable impression on so many potentially influential people.

24 THURSDAY *Moon Age Day 13 Moon Sign Gemini*

It looks as though Christmas Eve is likely to be something of a mixed bag for you, but you do have what it takes to make others sit up and take notice. Your opinions at the moment tend to be rather set and a little more flexibility would help. Present planetary trends make you very committed to family members.

25 FRIDAY *Moon Age Day 14 Moon Sign Gemini*

Christmas Day arrives and is going to bring with it a need for company. In turn, other people are apt to bring out the best in you, so a really intimate, family Christmas seems slightly less than likely. Be on your guard for any chance to break with usual routines and don't be frightened to ring those Christmas changes.

26 SATURDAY *Moon Age Day 15 Moon Sign Cancer*

This is a day during which you need to vent some of your pent-up frustrations. These can probably be dispersed simply by enjoying a change of scenery and by doing something different from the Christmas norm. If the weather is good you might opt for a walk in the country or by the coast. Whatever you choose, variety is essential.

27 SUNDAY *Moon Age Day 16 Moon Sign Cancer*

The way to stay happy today is through social matters and group encounters. Aries needs company right now and relishes the cut and thrust of interesting and stimulating conversation. Not everyone seems to be on your side, but you can easily brush off a few comments that seem custom-made to annoy you.

28 MONDAY *Moon Age Day 17 Moon Sign Leo*

You need more genuine fun and stimulating romance in your life at this time and the planets are likely to oblige. Entertaining others is as simple as encountering them in social situations or inviting them round to your home. Most people find you absolutely fascinating to have around and will be happy to tell you.

29 TUESDAY *Moon Age Day 18 Moon Sign Leo*

Most issues will be going your way, mainly because you are willing to take life by the scruff of the neck and shake it into what you want. There is a slightly ruthless streak about, but as long as you look out for the good of others, as well as feathering your own nest, this shouldn't be much of a problem.

30 WEDNESDAY *Moon Age Day 19 Moon Sign Virgo*

Your tongue and wit are both extremely sharp at present and whilst this is a very positive trend there is just a slight possibility that you could offer someone offence without realising you have done so. Maybe just a little more concern for the sensibilities of people in your vicinity is called for right now.

31 THURSDAY *Moon Age Day 20 Moon Sign Virgo*

Other people will certainly notice the speed with which you express yourself at the moment and more than a few of them want to be involved in your present ideas. Your mind is already well into the New Year and it is unlikely that you will be making too many resolutions. Aries knows what it wants and plans well ahead to get it.

ARIES:
2016 DIARY PAGES

ARIES: YOUR YEAR IN BRIEF

There is plenty to keep you occupied as this year begins, and you may spend the first week or two catching up with everything you were unable to do during the holidays. You should be in gear quite early in January and anxious to make new starts to coincide with the New Year. This trend continues throughout February. Friends should be especially helpful and colleagues will have plenty of input, too. Your romantic life may be a little topsy-turvy but any issues should be quickly resolved. You will also know instinctively how to do the right thing in a professional sense.

March and April should bring you closer to achieving a long-held desire. Of course there will be ups and downs, but the general mood is one of progress and satisfaction with your efforts. You will be even more boisterous than usual and more inclined to let people know exactly what you want from them. Avoid routines if you can at this time, you will feel they are a pointless distraction.

With the early summer comes a desire to break the bounds of the possible and to do something new. During May and June you will discover new things about yourself and will attempt things that might have barely seemed credible only a few months ago. People admire you, and you can show your appreciation by doing all you can to help friends. It isn't out of the question that a lifelong ambition can now be achieved.

By the time July comes along you will be feeling slightly restless, but still on pretty good form. You need stimulus and you won't take kindly to being held back in any way. There could be new offers at work, especially during August, which is another good month to escape your ties and do some travelling. It doesn't matter how far you go, it's your enthusiasm that counts.

Although you may be slightly less positive in your approach to life during the autumn, you will continue to display those typical Aries qualities that make you so good to be around. Do not underestimate any new, perhaps low-key, opportunities offered in September and October. Enjoy a good period for romance and say the right things to your partner at the most appropriate times.

The last two months of the year, November and December, are fairly positive especially in terms of personal attachments and money. Focus on your strengths during November, not your limitations. Although you might make mistakes, in the end you will be pleased with your results. Christmas should be a particularly enticing period this time around and the holidays might be magical.

January 2016

1 FRIDAY *Moon Age Day 21 Moon Sign Virgo*

Standard responses probably won't work very well today. You need to be willing to look at situations in a new and original way. If there is one zodiac sign that responds well to the demands of life it is yours. You remain adaptable, capable and well able to get ahead of the field throughout today.

2 SATURDAY *Moon Age Day 22 Moon Sign Libra*

Things could slow down noticeably today, mainly because the Moon has now moved into your opposite zodiac sign of Libra. This is the time of the month known as the 'lunar low' and it often finds you watching and waiting, rather than taking action. You might be quite happy this weekend to occupy your favourite and warmest chair.

3 SUNDAY *Moon Age Day 23 Moon Sign Libra*

It is unlikely that you will be pushing too hard in any direction for the moment. There is no harm whatsoever in taking time out to re-charge your batteries. Quieter pursuits might appeal to you and you should not, perhaps, expect to excel at sport for today at least. A new week will bring new pressures so make the most of this interlude.

4 MONDAY *Moon Age Day 24 Moon Sign Scorpio*

Trends continue to assist you to get ahead of the game and all it takes from you is some concentration – and some of that Aries genius! There should also be time today to make a fuss of family members, especially your partner. You remain inventive and can tell a tale as well as anyone in your circle.

5 TUESDAY *Moon Age Day 25 Moon Sign Scorpio*

You should find people around you supportive today and willing and able to offer you assistance. This trend is so strong it might all be too much to bear. You are used to coping with things yourself and you certainly don't need a nursemaid. You may be inclined to withdraw from situations that put you in someone's debt.

6 WEDNESDAY ☿ *Moon Age Day 26 Moon Sign Scorpio*

Standing up to bullies is something you do at every possible opportunity. What's more, you tend to show support for others who are under pressure because you hate to witness injustice. Today your charitable nature may come to the fore and most of what you do right now is for those around you.

7 THURSDAY ☿ *Moon Age Day 27 Moon Sign Sagittarius*

A tendency right now to rely on others won't please you very much because you prefer to be at the head of things and certainly don't want to think that anyone is offering you special treatment. Get out and about as much as you can today and don't allow yourself to be trapped in one place for hours on end. You need change and diversity.

8 FRIDAY ☿ *Moon Age Day 28 Moon Sign Sagittarius*

It is very important to remain focused today and to concentrate on specific issues rather than trying to get too much done at once. Look out for people who are in the know and learn from their obvious experience. There are some unusual times in store and you need to use all your intuition when it comes to decisions.

9 SATURDAY ☿ *Moon Age Day 0 Moon Sign Capricorn*

Today you apply yourself well to any challenge that comes your way. You might be feeling a little lethargic, especially if you have been pushing yourself hard recently. If this turns out to be the case you can rely on the good offices of colleagues and friends to help you along.

10 SUNDAY ☿ *Moon Age Day 1 Moon Sign Capricorn*

Don't wait for good things to turn up of their own accord. If you want to make progress socially this weekend you will need to take the lead. Organise a family meeting of some sort, or try to ensure that everyone eats together. If you take charge, things may turn out the way you want.

11 MONDAY ☿ *Moon Age Day 2 Moon Sign Aquarius*

Getting to grips with new incentives means paying attention, and that is something you might find a little difficult under present planetary trends. Your mind is inclined to wander and you won't have quite the level of concentration that is usually the case. All the same, today can be humorous and you should feel quite optimistic.

12 TUESDAY ☿ *Moon Age Day 3 Moon Sign Aquarius*

Now with a strong thirst for adventure you appear to be ploughing your way through January without stopping to take stock. At this time, you feel the need to move about as freely as you wish but you may be encumbered by circumstances and the winter weather. Take any opportunity to bring summer temporarily into your life.

13 WEDNESDAY ☿ *Moon Age Day 4 Moon Sign Pisces*

Keep in touch with people you don't see very often and use at least part of today to send emails or text messages and make telephone calls. You may also be taking time out to get up-to-speed with the latest technology and you may feel drawn towards puzzles or questions that appear to have no tangible answer.

14 THURSDAY ☿ *Moon Age Day 5 Moon Sign Pisces*

It may be time to focus on essential practical matters, probably for the first time this year. There are gains to be made at work or in any situation that finds you in congenial company. At work it looks as though you could be making great progress, even if you have to coax other, less motivated, people along the way.

15 FRIDAY ☿ *Moon Age Day 6 Moon Sign Pisces*

Disagreements at work come as a sharp contrast to the way things are turning out in your home life. Colleagues could be difficult to deal with or simply reluctant to do things in the way you would wish. A few compromises may be necessary and if that doesn't work it might be best simply to work on your own.

16 SATURDAY ☿ *Moon Age Day 7 Moon Sign Aries*

If you are working on this particular Saturday you should find things falling into place in just the way you would wish. Not much has changed this month, except for the fact that you are now so much more decisive than you may have been late last year. Lady Luck is on your side and that means you can throw caution to the wind.

17 SUNDAY ☿ *Moon Age Day 8 Moon Sign Aries*

The Moon is in Aries and that can make for a rip-roaring Sunday of fun and frolics. Unless you work at the weekend you will have time on your hands and you need to fill every second under this most impulsive trend. You would soon become impatient if others kicked their heels, and will be more organised than ever.

18 MONDAY ☿ *Moon Age Day 9 Moon Sign Taurus*

Certain financial matters might seem to be more trouble than they are worth, which is why you may decide to shelve such issues until later. Get to grips with an issue in your home life that needs sorting out but don't stick around in the same place all day. The more variety you get into your life the better you are likely to feel.

19 TUESDAY ☿ *Moon Age Day 10 Moon Sign Taurus*

Times change very quickly for Aries, it's part of the way you work as an individual. Now you are likely to be giving yourself exclusively to your work and you can make significant progress today. You will be very anxious to cut through any red tape that surrounds you and you will want to go straight to the heart of all issues.

20 WEDNESDAY ☿ *Moon Age Day 11 Moon Sign Gemini*

In practical matters there might be too much coming and going for your liking. Arians like to be sure of themselves and in command of all situations, and may become frustrated if this isn't always the case. Rest assured that even if you are discomfited, you are never far out of the picture and can easily keep up with the pace.

21 THURSDAY ☿ *Moon Age Day 12 Moon Sign Gemini*

If you are looking for friendship you can't go wrong under present planetary trends. Social situations look especially interesting and what happens this evening, in particular, could prove to be heart-warming and very enjoyable. With one eye on the weekend it looks as though you will be madly planning some sort of event.

22 FRIDAY ☿ *Moon Age Day 13 Moon Sign Cancer*

You are likely to be very focused on your financial goals today and will know how to make money, even if those around you seem determined to spend it. Try getting out and about with your friends and enjoy what life has to offer away from your own front door. The world can be your oyster under present planetary trends.

23 SATURDAY ☿ *Moon Age Day 14 Moon Sign Cancer*

Today's trends bring you good taste and the ability to express it quietly for the moment. It won't be hard for you to know instinctively what looks and feels right, either for yourself or for those you care about. You have time to listen to the genuine concerns of family members and may help to put things right for them.

24 SUNDAY ☿ *Moon Age Day 15 Moon Sign Leo*

This is a pretty good time for all intellectual pursuits and for showing everyone just how smart you can be. You won't have a lot of truck with rules and regulations just now and can easily become bored if you have to do the same old things time and again. Aim to make changes wherever possible – though not for the sake of it.

25 MONDAY ☿ *Moon Age Day 16 Moon Sign Leo*

Your mind is sharp and you undertake any sort of work quickly and with great efficiency. As a result you should get things done in half the usual time and will be waiting around for others to catch up. Accept that not everyone has your quick mind or your physical dexterity and exercise a little extra patience when required.

26 TUESDAY ☿ *Moon Age Day 17 Moon Sign Leo*

Be sensitive to the moods of others today but not to the extent that you allow them to drag you down if they happen to be depressed. You are the person who needs to keep everyone smiling and that means staying cheerful yourself. In many ways you are the natural clown of the zodiac now and are at your happiest when on the stage of life.

27 WEDNESDAY *Moon Age Day 18 Moon Sign Virgo*

Don't go in for impulse buying today because you could discover that what you thought was a bargain turns out to be quite the opposite. Give yourself time to listen to the opinions of family members and do what you can to support the underdog in any situation. Happiness comes today from being supportive to others.

28 THURSDAY *Moon Age Day 19 Moon Sign Virgo*

If it feels as though something is missing today you may need to be the one who searches it out. You are adaptable and positive and that means a time filled with possibilities. Even though this is the coldest month of the year you will want to get out of the house and do something exciting.

29 FRIDAY *Moon Age Day 20 Moon Sign Libra*

You may have to exercise some caution when it comes to material plans, otherwise you could fall foul of alterations or cancellations. Check all details, especially if you are travelling. Happily, Arians are very adaptable people and whatever happens today, you should manage to make the best of it.

30 SATURDAY *Moon Age Day 21 Moon Sign Libra*

Today you are good at using your mind in a very discriminating way and it would take someone extremely smart to pull the wool over your eyes. There is nothing strange about this for Aries but you will be extra perceptive under present trends. Some jobs may seem to take ages but you will get where you are going in the end.

31 SUNDAY *Moon Age Day 22 Moon Sign Libra*

You could feel more sensitive than usual and, if so, it is likely that you will see slights and insults where they were not intended. When Aries gets into this frame of mind virtually nobody can get them out of it. Distract yourself by trying something new. That way you won't have time to be glum.

February 2016

1 MONDAY *Moon Age Day 23 Moon Sign Scorpio*

The month may begin more slowly than you had anticipated. This is because all sorts of delays and little obstacles come along, all of which combine to make you slightly frustrated. If you accept that most of the problem exists in your mind you should avoid getting yourself into a stew about inconsequential matters.

2 TUESDAY *Moon Age Day 24 Moon Sign Scorpio*

For much of today you will be making your own decisions and avoiding the advice of your colleagues and friends, no matter how well intentioned it might be. You can't bear to think that people know more than you, which is a demonstration of the inherent Aries superiority. You may be correct – but try to be humble all the same.

3 WEDNESDAY *Moon Age Day 25 Moon Sign Sagittarius*

A relaxed attitude begins to develop, especially at work. When you are not toiling away you will find more time to socialise and may make new acquaintances. Be aware that there may be small financial gains to be made, mostly by being in the right place to pick up on new opportunities.

4 THURSDAY *Moon Age Day 26 Moon Sign Sagittarius*

Things should still be working out fairly well for you. There might be moments when you come across as being too pushy but in the case of those who know you well this won't be a problem. Trends suggest that new sporting activities or hobbies are possible now and you may also be more inclined to act on impulse.

5 FRIDAY *Moon Age Day 27 Moon Sign Sagittarius*

Give yourself a pat on the back for some of your present successes but don't allow anything to slow you down. It is vital that you keep going to the end of any task you take on because you don't need any loose ends under present trends. When work is out of the way you will respond well to the overtures of friends on a social level.

6 SATURDAY *Moon Age Day 28 Moon Sign Capricorn*

You still have a great capacity to mix business and pleasure – so much so that jobs that were a chore previously are now a positive joy. In general, people will love to have you around and may be showering compliments upon you. Your sense of humour is especially well tuned at this time and you won't be afraid to show what a practical joker you can be.

7 SUNDAY *Moon Age Day 29 Moon Sign Capricorn*

Just keep telling yourself that this is a Sunday and that you don't have to be doing something constructive all the time. It would suit present trends if you were to relax more and to do things that have no actual end product but which are intended for amusement only. Stand by for some startling revelations from a good friend.

8 MONDAY *Moon Age Day 0 Moon Sign Aquarius*

If there are annoying little interludes today you should be able to deal with these quite successfully. The first line of defence, if possible, is to remove yourself from the source of the irritation. Failing this you will have to steel yourself – even if the constant exposure to it feels like torture to you.

9 TUESDAY *Moon Age Day 1 Moon Sign Aquarius*

Confidence should not be in short supply today and with compliments coming your way from a host of different directions you can be absolutely sure of the popularity that surrounds you. You will also be quite efficient under present planetary trends and might achieve your chosen objectives in a fraction of the time even you would expect.

10 WEDNESDAY *Moon Age Day 2 Moon Sign Pisces*

It's time to get active – but you may have to accept that you don't have anywhere near enough time to do everything that demands your attention. This is where the art of delegation comes in and, believe it or not, other people can be quite capable if you allow them the chance! By evening you will be ready to rest.

11 THURSDAY *Moon Age Day 3 Moon Sign Pisces*

Keep away from noisy or troublesome types and don't get involved in situations that have nothing to do with you. By all means defend your friends and especially your partner, but don't dominate situations more than is strictly necessary. Confidence to do the right thing remains high but you don't rush in where angels fear to tread.

12 FRIDAY *Moon Age Day 4 Moon Sign Aries*

You can now afford to push your luck a little and you won't be at the back of the queue if you take the chance to push in near the front. Everyone wants to have you around and you are as bright and cheerful as you can be when in company. You should also be very romantically inclined and may gain admirers all day long.

13 SATURDAY *Moon Age Day 5 Moon Sign Aries*

Feelings of satisfaction attend your life today, probably because you have managed to do things during the week that will make you feel secure and settled. Beneath the surface of your mind is a wonderful place you can go in quieter moments and you seem to be well able to invent your own universe when you are relaxing.

14 SUNDAY *Moon Age Day 6 Moon Sign Taurus*

Life should continue to be interesting and you will also be responding well to the fact that the spring is just around the corner. Delays are possible today and certain arrangements might have to be altered at short notice. This should not trouble you but could be a source of concern to some of the people around you.

15 MONDAY *Moon Age Day 7 Moon Sign Taurus*

You may now have a considerable opportunity to make professional gains. You are at the start of a high-profile period during which your Aries nature will show itself to its best advantage. Steam ahead towards success and allow others to help you out if that is what they seem inclined to do. Don't worry about any minor aches and pains.

16 TUESDAY *Moon Age Day 8 Moon Sign Gemini*

Twosomes are probably where it's at for you right now. You get on best when co-operating with others in some way, whether this is in business or in your personal life. You will enjoy the fact that you can share things and at the same time the adage 'two heads are better than one' certainly seems to be the case as far as you are concerned.

17 WEDNESDAY *Moon Age Day 9 Moon Sign Gemini*

Communications may raise some unexpected and thought-provoking issues and you are undoubtedly in for some surprises in most areas of your life today. This would be a great time for making a spontaneous trip with your partner or a friend, but even if you have to travel on business you should make interesting discoveries along the way.

18 THURSDAY *Moon Age Day 10 Moon Sign Cancer*

Take the initiative where plans and schemes are concerned and don't leave them to the caprices of other people. The rest of the world won't necessarily have your energy or know-how and it is vitally important today that you feel yourself to be 'in command'. You may also encounter people you don't see very often.

19 FRIDAY *Moon Age Day 11 Moon Sign Cancer*

You may feel the need to seek out others today in your desire for greater excitement. You may be attracted to adventurous types who have a desire to break the bounds of the possible. Allied to such individuals you will become more daring yourself and may surprise yourself with your courage and dexterity.

20 SATURDAY *Moon Age Day 12 Moon Sign Cancer*

Try not to let anyone dominate your thoughts or actions at this time – not even your life partner. You really do know best when it comes to what is right for you. Be tactful with those who only have your best interests at heart, but remain determined. It would be far too easy today to simply capitulate.

21 SUNDAY *Moon Age Day 13 Moon Sign Leo*

Use today to put the force of your personality to good use and achieve singular objectives by being your usual decisive self. Fresh achievements may be made in any matter to do with education or where legacies are concerned. You may also find that you are somehow a lot more ingenious than is sometimes the case.

22 MONDAY *Moon Age Day 14 Moon Sign Leo*

You remain willing to exchange ideas with almost anyone but what you won't do is to admit that they are right and you are quite definitely wrong. There is an element of stubbornness here because there will always be occasions when you can learn from your mistakes. But you can't do so unless you are willing to admit they exist.

23 TUESDAY *Moon Age Day 15 Moon Sign Virgo*

Things might appear to become unstable and certain plans are likely to become unworkable at this time. Instead of throwing in the towel and abandoning them altogether it would be better to watch and wait for a while. It won't be more than a few hours before you are right back on form and anxious to get moving again.

24 WEDNESDAY *Moon Age Day 16 Moon Sign Virgo*

You are now a very stimulating person to be with and practically everything you do is sprinkled with magic. You approach all situations with a great deal of optimism and your warm personality shows through all the time. Most important of all is the fact that you are showing your concern for others in very tangible and practical ways.

25 THURSDAY *Moon Age Day 17 Moon Sign Libra*

The Moon has entered your opposite sign, bringing with it your monthly 'lunar low'. Take some time out for observation and put off things that could easily be done later, or not at all. Rely on family members and seek out your friends if you feel like having a chat. In this way you will ride out the trend.

26 FRIDAY *Moon Age Day 18 Moon Sign Libra*

As today advances you should gradually feel more and more energised, although it won't be until the end of the day that you are really back on form. You could delight in something that increases your knowledge and will also be showing the refined side of your nature. You won't take to showy or boastful people today.

27 SATURDAY *Moon Age Day 19 Moon Sign Libra*

Meeting people, travelling and learning from your experiences are all important components of this particular weekend. What matters the most is broadening your horizons and this is something you achieve without really having to try. Just imagine what else you could achieve if you really put your mind to something!

28 SUNDAY *Moon Age Day 20 Moon Sign Scorpio*

Today's trends make you adaptable and versatile and this can be put to good use in any number of ways. While others find life and situations to be complicated, you steam ahead and sort out problems as and when they occur. In affairs of the heart standard responses won't work well and a little more originality is called for.

29 MONDAY *Moon Age Day 21 Moon Sign Scorpio*

You may decide that you are not getting where you want to be in terms of your professional life and if this turns out to be the case you will have to make some fairly radical changes in the not too distant future. Getting your head round the motivations of those you are close to might be rather more difficult today than it is normally.

March 2016

1 TUESDAY *Moon Age Day 22 Moon Sign Sagittarius*

This may not be a straightforward time. People can be confused about what they want from you and without any real indication of how to proceed you will have to rely mainly on intuition. Fortunately this is not a problem for the sign of Aries right now, but you will have to be perceptive in your dealings with some relatives and friends.

2 WEDNESDAY *Moon Age Day 23 Moon Sign Sagittarius*

You have a great capacity to love at present and the depth of your feelings might prove a mystery to less emotional types. On the surface you often seem totally in command of yourself and people would never guess what a maelstrom might be spiralling away inside your heart. With excellent powers of communication you can now tell them.

3 THURSDAY *Moon Age Day 24 Moon Sign Sagittarius*

Love could still be uppermost in your mind. Aries people who are between relationships at the moment should keep their eyes and ears open because new possibilities seem to be at hand. You will also be much more inclined than usual to act on impulse and to move people with your honesty and disarming charm.

4 FRIDAY *Moon Age Day 25 Moon Sign Capricorn*

Don't be surprised if there is something 'odd' about today. You could be getting small but definite clues about your potential future behaviour, mostly from what other people are saying to you. Coincidences will probably abound and you may be able to make significant progress without the need to plan ahead as much as usual.

5 SATURDAY *Moon Age Day 26 Moon Sign Capricorn*

Keep up with news and views and pay particular attention to topical information that has a direct bearing on your life. It might be necessary to adapt in some way in order to accommodate what is happening on a regional or national level and you won't want to be left behind when it comes to discussions about what is happening in the world.

6 SUNDAY *Moon Age Day 27 Moon Sign Aquarius*

Free advice probably comes with a catch under present trends, so be wary of paying it too much attention. Get-rich-quick schemes should be avoided at all costs because, as you would normally realise, very few of them have any merit at all. Aries is almost never gullible but there is just a chance you could be taken in at this time.

7 MONDAY *Moon Age Day 28 Moon Sign Aquarius*

Your mind is inclined to turn towards career matters around this time, and you will most likely have new and better incentives to put in extra effort and to think situations through in revolutionary ways. Friends should be especially warm and supportive at this time and your social life may include many 'fun' situations.

8 TUESDAY *Moon Age Day 0 Moon Sign Pisces*

If responsibilities get in the way of your freedom you should create islands of time in which you don't even think about what is expected of you. Having fun at the moment doesn't mean achieving anything concrete and you merely need to enjoy yourself. Friends should be willing to help when it comes to some challenging possibilities.

9 WEDNESDAY *Moon Age Day 1 Moon Sign Pisces*

Life should be quite progressive at this time and things will fall into place of their own accord – if you only allow them the chance to do so. You could begin to see patterns developing that you never noticed before and there is something unusual about the number of random chance events firing off around you during this period.

10 THURSDAY *Moon Age Day 2 Moon Sign Aries*

Now all your energy comes into its own and the 'lunar high' offers you brand new incentives and a positive attitude that cannot be underestimated. It is possible that you may be lucky with money if you exercise caution and use your common sense, and that you will be quick to recognise any potential advantage.

11 FRIDAY *Moon Age Day 3 Moon Sign Aries*

You will want to be on the move all day and that means organising yourself properly. Thinking on your feet is not at all hard but you can miss so much if you are not prepared. You would probably enjoy a spending spree at the moment and you certainly will not want to waste the day sitting around.

12 SATURDAY *Moon Age Day 4 Moon Sign Taurus*

If you are not at first able to capitalise on your ideas you might be left feeling frustrated. It's time to explain yourself carefully and to make certain that colleagues, in particular, have a good understanding of what you are talking about. Reactions may be mixed, but you may not need to be thwarted by people who won't keep up.

13 SUNDAY *Moon Age Day 5 Moon Sign Taurus*

Originality is vitally important to Aries people. You never want to be just one of the herd and you are only really happy when you are out in front. You have fewer chances to be a trailblazer at the moment but you are like a snake, coiled for action and waiting to strike. Organise a family outing today and leave practical matters until later.

14 MONDAY *Moon Age Day 6 Moon Sign Gemini*

If responsibilities are getting in the way of your free time there ought to be ways in which you can find the fun element in some of your duties. Think in terms of games rather than chores and everything should fall into place. Your sense of humour is very keen at the moment and you will enjoy a practical joke, either on you or by you.

15 TUESDAY *Moon Age Day 7 Moon Sign Gemini*

This should be a period of high enthusiasm and a time when you are showing your best face to the world at large. Not everything interests you today, but most matters will. It can be extraordinarily fascinating to get to know others, particularly when you are dealing with people who have a mysterious side to their nature.

16 WEDNESDAY *Moon Age Day 8 Moon Sign Gemini*

The atmosphere at home ought to be particularly stimulating at this time. There is much in your chart this month that ties you to family members, but the more gregarious and out-going side of your nature is also to the fore. Trying to establish the best of both worlds, domestic bliss and worldly experience, may not be easy.

17 THURSDAY *Moon Age Day 9 Moon Sign Cancer*

A boost to communication comes along at this time. That means you will be busy, out there in the wider world, talking to as many people as possible. Rather nervous at present, you may chatter too much, but people don't mind because you always have something interesting to say.

18 FRIDAY *Moon Age Day 10 Moon Sign Cancer*

If you find there are pressures building at home it might be best to get out of the house with your partner or friends. Give and take in personal matters is essential and you really do need to listen to what important people are saying. Some genuine intimacy in the evening would be more than welcome.

19 SATURDAY *Moon Age Day 11 Moon Sign Leo*

The go-getting side of your nature shows itself this weekend. You find communicating with others easier than usual because you are meeting more people with whom you can strike up a conversation. Get yourself into a positive frame of mind regarding family commitments. You might also decide to take a journey today.

20 SUNDAY *Moon Age Day 12 Moon Sign Leo*

Social matters continue to be quite rewarding and you won't find it hard to get on with anyone around you. When you need to organise something, plan well in advance, get some expert advice and be willing to accept help when it is offered. A really good friend has something quite special to tell you.

21 MONDAY *Moon Age Day 13 Moon Sign Virgo*

Socially speaking you have every opportunity to be yourself. Always the life and soul of the party, you can also help others to have a good time. One of your best qualities at the moment is your ability to bring out the best in someone who has been going through a very hard time in the recent past.

22 TUESDAY *Moon Age Day 14 Moon Sign Virgo*

Your way of enjoying life now is directly related to your desire to broaden your horizons. Travel is probably on your mind, together with changes you want to make around your home. This may be the first time this year that you really take note of the changing seasons and the way they make you feel.

23 WEDNESDAY *Moon Age Day 15 Moon Sign Virgo*

You could feel under pressure at present to keep on top of practical matters. Don't take on too many varied responsibilities but stick in the main to what you understand. You always feel the need to break down barriers, but accept that you don't have to be doing so all the time. Today requires rest.

24 THURSDAY *Moon Age Day 16 Moon Sign Libra*

Life will slow down at this time and you will have to accept it. Aries doesn't respond as well to the 'lunar low' as some of the other zodiac signs. You can't stand the thought that you suddenly have to slacken your pace, and you tend to go on putting in masses of effort, much of which will be wasted.

25 FRIDAY *Moon Age Day 17 Moon Sign Libra*

Attracting the right sort of advice may be easier now because you are slowed down enough to take notice of it. Use today for conversation and for learning new things. Don't try to achieve too much in the practical world and don't expect to excel when it comes to sport or other physical activities.

26 SATURDAY *Moon Age Day 18 Moon Sign Scorpio*

Capitalising on every single opportunity that life offers you is what your zodiac sign is all about. That is especially true at the moment and you clearly have all that it takes to get the very best out of life. What might prove to be difficult are personal attachments because people just don't understand you now.

27 SUNDAY *Moon Age Day 19 Moon Sign Scorpio*

It is almost certain that there will be some delays today, but since Sunday is supposed to be a day of rest, maybe this won't bother you too much. Stand back and watch life happening, something you rarely do. Confidence is absent in some matters, but in others you feel well up to the task.

28 MONDAY *Moon Age Day 20 Moon Sign Scorpio*

You will have to focus on little jobs today, even though doing so isn't exactly easy. The fact is that you want to be up and away, but mundane aspects of life keep calling you back. Pay attention to what you are doing, even if this isn't easy, or risk making some serious mistakes.

29 TUESDAY *Moon Age Day 21 Moon Sign Sagittarius*

You are in a big hurry to achieve material objectives and to get to all those things in life that you really want. What you need to realise is that this is the way nature made you. Go steadily, plan carefully and, in the end, you can obtain most of what your heart desires. But you will always want more – that's Aries.

30 WEDNESDAY *Moon Age Day 22 Moon Sign Sagittarius*

There is a danger that you could be rather too impetuous regarding a money or work-based matter so take time to think things through. If certain aspects of your daily routine are becoming repetitive, vary your life in small ways and do things in a different order. You will still get everything done, but things will feel fresher.

31 THURSDAY *Moon Age Day 23 Moon Sign Capricorn*

A change of scene would doubtless suit you down to the ground and offers you the necessary stimulus that you really want in your life right now. Confidence is strong, especially when you know that you are making progress in your life. Attitude is all-important when you are dealing with superiors or people new to you.

April

2016

1 FRIDAY *Moon Age Day 24 Moon Sign Capricorn*

It's April Fool's Day, but aside from the fact that you are naturally inclined towards practical jokes, you are certainly no fool today. Matters associated with your love life continue to be rewarding, offering you plenty to write home about and a greater degree of self-worth. Attitude is all-important today.

2 SATURDAY *Moon Age Day 25 Moon Sign Capricorn*

Someone could be proving very reluctant when it comes to making their own decisions. You can't live people's lives for them but it may be possible for you to exert a significant influence. Confidence is still present in great measure, especially in any situation where you are selling a commodity – or yourself.

3 SUNDAY *Moon Age Day 26 Moon Sign Aquarius*

You should be in high spirits today and keen to mix and mingle as much as you can. Although there are still one or two frustrations about, mainly coming from the direction of others, relationships on a personal level should be good and your ability to speak your mind certainly isn't in doubt.

4 MONDAY *Moon Age Day 27 Moon Sign Aquarius*

This is a good period for reflecting on recent progress and for laying down plans for the future. In a few days the 'lunar high' will bring all the incentive you could need, which is why clearing the decks for action at the moment is so essential. Don't expect to be the life and soul of any party, at least for now.

5 TUESDAY *Moon Age Day 28 Moon Sign Pisces*

Excellent things are happening on a practical level now. There could be some financial luck and a better than average ability to attract money to yourself. Socially speaking you will be on good form but will get on best of all with those individuals to whom you have a special attachment, particularly your partner.

6 WEDNESDAY *Moon Age Day 29 Moon Sign Pisces*

Some jobs are a real chore but you will feel obliged to get on with them, at least early in the day. Keep a sense of proportion when dealing with the demands of family members, but do be on hand if you are needed. Today represents a time when you will want to show the world how versatile you can be.

7 THURSDAY *Moon Age Day 0 Moon Sign Aries*

The Moon returns to your zodiac sign and is supported there by a host of other planetary positions. This is a day during which you are taking the lead and also finding within yourself the friendly qualities that may have been lacking of late. Progress is the name of the game, making for a fascinating period.

8 FRIDAY *Moon Age Day 1 Moon Sign Aries*

You can still have your own way with others quite easily, though you do need to bear in mind that their opinions won't necessarily be the same as yours. Concerning yourself with the practical in life won't matter so much at a time when you simply want to have fun. Diversion is the name of the game today.

9 SATURDAY *Moon Age Day 2 Moon Sign Taurus*

In social encounters you are the centre of attention and can get other people on your side when it proves to be necessary. There's a strong 'research' element about your mentality at the moment and a desire to know how and why things work in the way that they do. This could be a very enterprising and interesting day.

10 SUNDAY *Moon Age Day 3 Moon Sign Taurus*

Big ideas can be put into operation now and you should be pleased that you have taken time to put the plans in place in the recent past. Arguing your corner is something you do instinctively right now because you know that much of the future depends on starting down the right road in the first place.

11 MONDAY *Moon Age Day 4 Moon Sign Gemini*

Despite the planetary necessity of getting ahead practically speaking, there are other trends that point more towards your personal and romantic life. Make time to tell someone how much they mean to you and be prepared to make a real fuss of particular individuals. Socially speaking you ought to be on top form.

12 TUESDAY *Moon Age Day 5 Moon Sign Gemini*

With a tendency to feel less than inspired you have to be certain of your footing in almost everything today. Perhaps you feel the need to rest and to recharge your batteries. Certainly trying to plough ahead with specific projects may not be very easy and it may be better to let things ride for now.

13 WEDNESDAY *Moon Age Day 6 Moon Sign Cancer*

Jumping about from one foot to another is not typical of your zodiac sign but that is the way things will be for the moment. If you are indecisive you give others the wrong impression so it might be best to avoid making decisions at all, unless circumstances force you to do so. Keep a sense of proportion.

14 THURSDAY *Moon Age Day 7 Moon Sign Cancer*

Try to vary your routines as much as possible today. It is easy for you to become bored at present and you need as much variety as you can manage. The social side of life appeals to you the most and offers you the chance to bring change and diversity into your life. Plan now for an active and enterprising sort of weekend later.

15 FRIDAY *Moon Age Day 8 Moon Sign Leo*

New input comes your way, so whatever else you do, avoid keeping your ears closed right now. There are possible gains for the taking at work, with colleagues and superiors alike more than willing to lend a hand. Aries is in for a treat or two but just make sure you don't look any sort of gift horse in the mouth.

16 SATURDAY *Moon Age Day 9 Moon Sign Leo*

Whatever you do makes a great difference this weekend. You don't have to move mountains to let others know you are around. Your general frame of mind is positive and you are now constantly thinking up new ways to get ahead. Saturday brings you many chances to have fun and to avoid taking life too seriously.

17 SUNDAY *Moon Age Day 10 Moon Sign Virgo*

Although you are generally on a roll in your life at the moment, you shouldn't take everything you hear at face value. If there is one day of the month on which you could easily be duped, that day is here. You will want to give good value for money in your dealing with the world at large, even if you have to put yourself out.

18 MONDAY *Moon Age Day 11 Moon Sign Virgo*

Financially speaking this could be quite a taxing period, which means you should keep a close eye on where the pennies are going. Avoid lavish expenditure in any direction and, if possible, spend little or nothing until after tomorrow. It isn't quite so easy now to realise when people are trying to take advantage of you.

19 TUESDAY *Moon Age Day 12 Moon Sign Virgo*

Along comes a day when it ought to be more than possible to do your own thing. You won't take kindly to being told what to do, or how to go about it. Aries can be quite touchy at the moment and there are occasions when you may need to bite your tongue to avoid spoiling your chances for later.

20 WEDNESDAY *Moon Age Day 13 Moon Sign Libra*

This is a day when it would be better to pace yourself and not one on which you should go for gold in any way. The 'lunar low' has a bearing on most of your actions and can lead to unusual depressive feelings. Counter these trends by staying active, though in a low-key way, and by mixing with interesting people.

21 THURSDAY *Moon Age Day 14 Moon Sign Libra*

You demonstrate a quick wit and a tendency to fire back quickly today, though without any venom and with lots of humour. At heart you are a real old softie and ought to be more than willing to help out whenever you can. Charity work or community projects may appeal to you around this time.

22 FRIDAY *Moon Age Day 15 Moon Sign Libra*

The pace of progress picks up today after recent delays. Working slowly but definitely towards your objectives you ought to be more fired up with enthusiasm and quite happy to ring the changes socially. At work you should be making significant headway and will be anxious to show what you are made of.

23 SATURDAY ☿ *Moon Age Day 16 Moon Sign Scorpio*

Don't expect everyone to agree with your ideas at present. There are people around whose opinions are radically different from yours and there is little chance of you getting your own way in the end. The more conciliatory you are, the more likely you will be to make unexpected gains, and a few new friends on the way.

24 SUNDAY ☿ *Moon Age Day 17 Moon Sign Scorpio*

Socially speaking you find yourself reaching a peak and you are more than willing to rub shoulders with new people who come into your life. There is a distinct possibility that you could be making friends who will stay around for a long time to come. Good pals are hard to come by, so keep your eyes open.

25 MONDAY ☿ *Moon Age Day 18 Moon Sign Sagittarius*

This is a time when you can get things organised and during which you are clearly in the market for a challenge. Although the new week might bring social demands, you are still able to look practical matters squarely in the face. Hard work is something that doesn't frighten you in the least, as you are about to discover.

26 TUESDAY ☿ *Moon Age Day 19 Moon Sign Sagittarius*

This is a key moment in terms of finances. You need to look carefully at what you are spending and, if necessary, avoid parting with cash at all for today. There are some real bargains around the corner and you would only kick yourself if you committed yourself to great expenditure and then discovered your mistake later.

27 WEDNESDAY ☿ *Moon Age Day 20 Moon Sign Capricorn*

A high-energy interlude is at hand. Many Aries people will be testing themselves physically and taking on new challenges. That's fine, but you don't have to push yourself to the limit. Arrangements have to be made that ensure your loved ones realise just how much you care for them in a moment-by-moment sense.

28 THURSDAY ☿ *Moon Age Day 21 Moon Sign Capricorn*

Any matters associated with communication should work out rather well today. You can also expect a social high-point, with offers coming in from a number of different directions. Your popularity brings you a lot of enjoyment now, and there's nothing that suits your zodiac sign more than that.

29 FRIDAY ☿ *Moon Age Day 22 Moon Sign Capricorn*

Ingenuity is now the way to success. Don't take anything at face value and if some of your original ideas are being shunned, it's up to you to explain yourself over again. Don't take no for an answer, especially on those occasions when you know very well you are right in what you are saying. Your creative potential looks good.

30 SATURDAY ☿ *Moon Age Day 23 Moon Sign Aquarius*

Today's pace of life may turn out much faster than you had expected. Little jobs get out of hand and the demands that others make of you come thick and fast. Despite all this you find the light of love is shining on you today, and you can find exactly the right words to put others at their ease.

May 2016

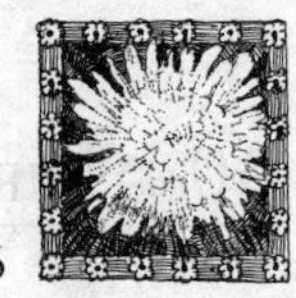

1 SUNDAY ☿ *Moon Age Day 24 Moon Sign Aquarius*

You may feel optimistic and adventurous today and it's an odds-on certainty that you will be trying to get to the end of a specific objective that you think has been waiting in the wings too long. There is a danger that you will rush things, so a little caution would be advisable no matter what you find yourself doing.

2 MONDAY ☿ *Moon Age Day 25 Moon Sign Pisces*

Don't allow unnecessary arguments to crop up and avoid getting on the wrong side of those who could be in the best position to support your present ideas. You may have to modify your stance regarding a family matter but once you have had time to think things through you will be able to see how sensible compromise actually is.

3 TUESDAY ☿ *Moon Age Day 26 Moon Sign Pisces*

Daily outings and even long-distance travel can be quite enjoyable at this time and you can achieve a great deal by putting yourself in the way of success, rather than by just hoping for it. Even little things can mean a lot to your nearest and dearest so put aside a little time to fuss round them or to say something unbidden and kind.

4 WEDNESDAY ☿ *Moon Age Day 27 Moon Sign Aries*

In a professional sense you won't have to look too hard for success while the 'lunar high' is around but the chances are that much of your attention is now focused on your personal and social life. Anything that means positive change and interaction with others is grist to your mill and you move forward with great hope.

5 THURSDAY ☿ *Moon Age Day 28 Moon Sign Aries*

Put your luck to the test right now and watch how things begin to pan out so positively for you. This is not a day to be stuck in the shadows or to remain within your own four walls. If you want to make the best of the 'lunar high' you need to be out there pitching. If that means putting yourself on display than so much the better.

6 FRIDAY ☿ *Moon Age Day 0 Moon Sign Taurus*

A fresh boost to love and romantic matters generally is supplied by the present position of the Moon. You will enjoy taking the starring role in life around this time and giving your best, particularly in social situations. Part of the reason you are so popular is that you have a great knack for saying and doing the right thing.

7 SATURDAY ☿ *Moon Age Day 1 Moon Sign Taurus*

Instead of being on the move again today you might choose to stick around and get on with all those jobs that have been piling up. You can be very efficient at the moment and willing to get to grips with tasks you had previously been avoiding. Friends have much to tell you and may impart some information you find especially intriguing.

8 SUNDAY ☿ *Moon Age Day 2 Moon Sign Gemini*

You are optimistic that anything you decide to undertake today will work out more or less as you might wish. You continue to make progress with new ideas and won't take no for an answer when you have made your mind up about anything. This could make you a little awkward to deal with around now.

9 MONDAY ☿ *Moon Age Day 3 Moon Sign Gemini*

In a social sense you will want to branch out this week and you won't be specifically tied to doing those things that routine demands. On the contrary you are breaking down the bounds of the commonplace and standing up for variety. This might not please everyone but with your silver tongue you can easily talk others round.

10 TUESDAY ☿ *Moon Age Day 4 Moon Sign Cancer*

Large enterprises or work on a scale you haven't encountered for a while should prove to be fortuitous and could lead you to a new level of success. Some of the ideas that occurred to you in the past are likely to replay themselves in your mind and you may find they are now more attainable.

11 WEDNESDAY ☿ *Moon Age Day 5 Moon Sign Cancer*

Social and teamwork matters are now even more highly emphasised than was the case yesterday. If you are a sporting Aries you could do well today, especially if you are involved in contact sports or are a member of a team. In a more practical sense you may need to remind yourself that everything that glistens is not gold.

12 THURSDAY ☿ *Moon Age Day 6 Moon Sign Leo*

Focus on your inner life for a while and look carefully at your deepest thoughts and emotions. This is a very good day to work out how your smallest actions can have a bearing on the lives of those around you. You may feel concern, not only for your immediate circle but also for your country and even the whole planet.

13 FRIDAY ☿ *Moon Age Day 7 Moon Sign Leo*

Today's trends bring you powers of attraction. It isn't hard for you to make friends and influence people at the best of times but right now your skills are amazing. Make use of this to further your ambitions at work, and once the daily grind is out of the way get together with like-minded people to have some fun.

14 SATURDAY ☿ *Moon Age Day 8 Moon Sign Leo*

Take a close look at the domestic scene and spend more time with family members and especially with your partner. It might seem as though there are few moments to spare in your busy schedule but you can always spare a moment for a cuddle and a few kind words. Under present trends these will mean a great deal.

15 SUNDAY ☿ *Moon Age Day 9 Moon Sign Virgo*

Right now you are very socially motivated and you have what it takes to make many new friends. People who have been on the periphery of your circle may now become more important and you could discover some facts about particular individuals that will surprise and maybe even shock you a little.

16 MONDAY ☿ *Moon Age Day 10 Moon Sign Virgo*

You are able to create a pleasant atmosphere wherever you go and with this long and positive period of sociability still going your way it looks as though you will get much of what you want from life without having to try too hard. People are virtually queuing up to get to know you, which is great for Aries.

17 TUESDAY ☿ *Moon Age Day 11 Moon Sign Libra*

You may be curious to know how something is working out beneath the surface, and so may do a little detective work around now. If you need to burn the candle at both ends do so today while you have sufficient energy because you will be much more withdrawn by tomorrow. Keep a sense of proportion regarding cash.

18 WEDNESDAY ☿ *Moon Age Day 12 Moon Sign Libra*

Some setbacks and alterations to plans will be inevitable whilst the 'lunar low' is around but this doesn't mean you have lie low. Just pace yourself and delegate when you need to. After all, you work hard enough for others at times, so you may find they are glad of the chance to reciprocate.

19 THURSDAY ☿ *Moon Age Day 13 Moon Sign Libra*

Although you could be feeling slightly insecure around now there is really no reason why this should be the case. In personal attachments it seems you have to work extremely hard to get others to compromise and life can seem just a little messy at times. By tomorrow many of your present concerns will have disappeared.

20 FRIDAY ☿ *Moon Age Day 14 Moon Sign Scorpio*

Be prepared for today to bring you a lesson in subtlety and for the dawning realisation that you haven't been quite as clever as you may have thought across the last few days. All the same, you remain popular and in demand socially, even though you might prefer the quiet life now.

21 SATURDAY ☿ *Moon Age Day 15 Moon Sign Scorpio*

You should be working hard and conscientiously but that may not be enough to get you ahead of the game at the moment. There may be someone around who has more experience or a greater level of influence and that could annoy you no end. Try not to let your jealousy show and you could still win the race in the end.

22 SUNDAY ☿ *Moon Age Day 16 Moon Sign Sagittarius*

You have great persuasive talents at the moment and if there is something you really want from life, this is probably the best time of the month to ask for it. Your skill is evident across the board, especially in any situation that finds you pitted against a competitor. You would be very unlikely to lose out in sporting activities now.

23 MONDAY *Moon Age Day 17 Moon Sign Sagittarius*

Promising news is likely to arrive around now and you will be happy to follow up on actions you took late last week. Newer and better possibilities at work come about not only as a result of your own actions but because others have been watching you carefully and will be working strongly on your behalf.

24 TUESDAY *Moon Age Day 18 Moon Sign Sagittarius*

Your actions bring out the co-operative instincts in others, both in the workplace and in more social activities. At the same time part of your mind is geared towards personal comfort and security. That's why you may be spending more time at home right now and also why you are planning to make certain specific changes.

25 WEDNESDAY *Moon Age Day 19 Moon Sign Capricorn*

You could be under pressure to get through a demanding work agenda, but unfortunately there is a part of you that isn't really interested in work right now. You may long for wide, open spaces and the chance to enjoy the late spring weather to the full. Find some time to take a walk, even if it's only to the nearest park.

26 THURSDAY *Moon Age Day 20 Moon Sign Capricorn*

Mars is one of the dominant forces in your solar chart at present. It increases your energy, offers newer and better incentives and shows you to be shrewd in your attitude. There isn't any doubting the level of your intelligence and others won't take you for granted. That's mainly because you won't allow them to do so.

27 FRIDAY *Moon Age Day 21 Moon Sign Aquarius*

From a social point of view things are running so smoothly that you might actively throw a spanner in the works just to see what happens. There's no doubt that you can be very mischievous right now, and your sense of fun is in full swing. Confidence remains high when you know what is expected of you.

28 SATURDAY *Moon Age Day 22 Moon Sign Aquarius*

The opportunity to express your affection comes all the time under present trends and you certainly won't be backward when it comes to uttering words of love and devotion. People actively want to have you around because they find you fun to be with and always optimistic. Money matters should also be stronger now.

29 SUNDAY *Moon Age Day 23 Moon Sign Pisces*

Be just a little careful this Sunday because it looks as though you could be outmanoeuvred by someone, maybe in terms of a financial opportunity. Your luck remains generally good but a slightly quieter approach is possible bearing in mind the current temporary planetary trends. You may feel a tendency to retreat somewhat.

30 MONDAY *Moon Age Day 24 Moon Sign Pisces*

You may feel strongly driven romantically and much of your energy today could be focused on your love life. With everything to play for in the romantic stakes you seem to make the best impression possible. This is especially true in the case of Aries people who are between romances or walking the path for the very first time.

31 TUESDAY *Moon Age Day 25 Moon Sign Pisces*

More than ever you yearn for freedom on this particular spring Tuesday and the call of the wild will be strong in your mind and heart. You need to change things in order to avoid feeling that life is becoming somehow routine. There's nothing strange about this as far as Aries is concerned, as you will already know.

June 2016

1 WEDNESDAY *Moon Age Day 26 Moon Sign Aries*

The 'lunar high' brings out the best in you in almost every way. You should be enthusiastic, expansive and very cheerful. All in all it is just possible that the power of your nature will be too much for some people. This is probably why you will spend more time with like-minded types during today and maybe into tomorrow.

2 THURSDAY *Moon Age Day 27 Moon Sign Aries*

Think big and expect only the best because that is what is likely to be coming your way at the moment. There won't be time to do everything, but you can make a solid impression at work and again in the evening at social gatherings. People will want you to take the lead and it won't be difficult to accommodate them.

3 FRIDAY *Moon Age Day 28 Moon Sign Taurus*

You probably can't complain that life is boring right now – in fact the opposite could be the case because you could need to slow things down a little. It's not that you are becoming fatigued but merely that you could be losing touch with some possibilities because you can't keep so many balls in the air at the same time.

4 SATURDAY *Moon Age Day 0 Moon Sign Taurus*

Your home life is apt to be rather busy, thanks to the present position of the Moon. It is possible that certain family members will be coming to a very important stage in their lives and they will be turning to you for advice. Whatever is going on you have what it takes to offer support and lend assistance.

5 SUNDAY *Moon Age Day 1 Moon Sign Gemini*

Today is a bonus as far as personal attachments are concerned. Romantic matters are emphasised and those Arians who have been looking for love should concentrate their efforts around now. In most situations you reveal yourself to be very idealistic and you won't compromise your principles – no matter what.

6 MONDAY *Moon Age Day 2 Moon Sign Gemini*

You will particularly enjoy being around people who give you encouragement and new incentives but you won't take kindly to associating with those who insist on being pessimistic. More than usual you are now very susceptible to atmospheres and need to seek out the most positive company that life can offer you.

7 TUESDAY *Moon Age Day 3 Moon Sign Cancer*

Show a little willpower and curb a tendency to eat or drink more than you know is good for you. Some Arians will be starting a health kick around now and if you are one of them just remember to proceed with caution instead of knocking yourself out on the first day. Rules and regulations don't sit well with you today.

8 WEDNESDAY *Moon Age Day 4 Moon Sign Cancer*

With enough insight you can solve tough problems and persuade others to follow your lead. In a personal sense you also have what it takes to turn heads and so you can expect to be popular right now. You achieve a really good understanding of what makes those around you tick and that can be useful.

9 THURSDAY *Moon Age Day 5 Moon Sign Leo*

Continuing on a generally positive journey through life this month you can now expect professional advancement as well as the accolades that may be bestowed by those in positions of authority. Although you will be more than justifying your position at work, quite a lot of your thinking time will be given over to home-based matters.

10 FRIDAY *Moon Age Day 6 Moon Sign Leo*

When it comes to general progress in life there is really nobody about to beat you. Your actions are dynamic and your thought processes will be clear and concise. While other people are thinking about doing something you will have it finished and be well on with the next task. Growth is the inevitable result.

11 SATURDAY *Moon Age Day 7 Moon Sign Virgo*

You are definitely in a mood for give and take, though there will be occasions when you expect more give from others and consequently more take from you. If someone accuses you, in a guarded way, of being a little selfish maybe you should think about what they are saying. You can get your own way but do it kindly and diplomatically.

12 SUNDAY *Moon Age Day 8 Moon Sign Virgo*

Avoid self-deception or any escapist tendencies and stick to what you know in a practical sense. There are times when you may feel yourself to be disorganised or unclear about the way things are going in a general sense. These interludes are now inevitable but they don't need to get in your way too much.

13 MONDAY *Moon Age Day 9 Moon Sign Virgo*

Career rewards may now result from the recognition of others of your professionalism and sense of fair play. You are likely to be feted by those who can do you some good and your responses remain extremely positive. Something you need to look for may turn out to be easier to find than you expect.

14 TUESDAY *Moon Age Day 10 Moon Sign Libra*

This is not an ideal day for taking on too many laborious tasks. Just go with the flow and let others do what they want. If you have time to yourself this evening, so much the better. Simply curl up in your favourite chair with a good book or watch some light television. The break will do you no end of good.

15 WEDNESDAY *Moon Age Day 11 Moon Sign Libra*

The power you have to change things in your life is limited under the 'lunar low' and there are times today when you will have to settle for second best. You want to be at the centre of things but situations get away from you and other people may seem to be reaping the rewards. Take comfort from the fact that these trends are temporary.

16 THURSDAY *Moon Age Day 12 Moon Sign Scorpio*

Today brings a very good period for working in conjunction with others and you may be surrounded by positive influences. The ideas of a friend might look particularly attractive and, for once, you are willing to let someone else take command. Well that's how it might look but of course you know different!

17 FRIDAY *Moon Age Day 13 Moon Sign Scorpio*

Business negations should go particularly well today and you should be on the ball when it comes to getting something you really want in a material sense. Not everyone favours your ideas but the dissenters can be brought round with a little charm. Journeys of one sort or another will be in the offing.

18 SATURDAY *Moon Age Day 14 Moon Sign Scorpio*

A helping hand may be required and you will be the first in the queue to offer all the support you can, especially to friends and family. You might be slightly off the ball when it comes to your intuition at home but when your instinct fails it looks as though you will have everyday common sense to take its place.

19 SUNDAY *Moon Age Day 15 Moon Sign Sagittarius*

You should find that your domestic and family life is where most of your attention tends to be focused at the moment – mainly because things that are happening out there in the wider world can seem somewhat threatening. Fortunately this is a temporary trend and within hours you should be more or less back to normal.

20 MONDAY *Moon Age Day 16 Moon Sign Sagittarius*

Your work life might be an area of pressure, which is unusual for Aries. Maybe you are trying to do too much or it could be that colleagues seem to be conspiring against you. Be aware that the slightly odd position of Mars could make you react without thinking things through and, in all probability, your fears are groundless.

21 TUESDAY *Moon Age Day 17 Moon Sign Capricorn*

You are now strongly motivated to be helpful and will be quite willing to put the interests of co-workers ahead of your own. That's the way to see things from one angle, but it is also possible that you are willing to coerce your way to the top if it proves to be necessary. Aries is a shrewd cookie, as you are about to prove.

22 WEDNESDAY *Moon Age Day 18 Moon Sign Capricorn*

Today you will continue to bring out the best in other people and can demonstrate the secret of your popularity at all social gatherings. You also have exactly what it takes to make the right impression in romantic settings. Nobody does it better than you do now when it comes to speaking the right words in loving situations.

23 THURSDAY *Moon Age Day 19 Moon Sign Aquarius*

You can derive pleasure from just about any form of travel today and will accept the chance to make a journey, no matter where the destination may be. What's more you can meet some fascinating people when you are away from your normal haunts and there is a good chance that an acquaintance made soon will become a firm friend.

24 FRIDAY *Moon Age Day 20 Moon Sign Aquarius*

Group matters work in your favour and you can once again prove just how positive you are when it comes to working in a team. As usual you soon rise to the top of the pile and though you genuinely do want equality you nearly always end up being first amongst equals. You will particularly enjoy stimulating conversations today.

25 SATURDAY *Moon Age Day 21 Moon Sign Aquarius*

You may now have fun at social functions and in any situation where your powers of communication can be put to the test. This is going to be a weekend of exciting opportunities. Some of these may turn out to be disappointing but there is always the next option to which you can turn and so you remain optimistic.

26 SUNDAY *Moon Age Day 22 Moon Sign Pisces*

It is very important to be fully aware of your motives today. It doesn't matter much why you do what you do but the result can be very important. If you recognise that you are being a little selfish, be honest with yourself and decide if the outcome justifies the means for yourself and colleagues and friends too.

27 MONDAY *Moon Age Day 23 Moon Sign Pisces*

This is the start of a week during which you may have to make some important career decisions. It's possible that some Aries types will be taking on new responsibilities and a change in direction isn't out of the question. Take some time to think things through and don't act entirely on impulse, at least not for now.

28 TUESDAY *Moon Age Day 24 Moon Sign Aries*

Certain goals and objectives are going to be much easier to achieve now whilst the 'lunar high' is around. There is little to hold you back and everything to play for, especially when it comes to love and romance. Make up your own rules and set out your stall to be a winner because that's the way the world sees you.

29 WEDNESDAY *Moon Age Day 25 Moon Sign Aries*

Your personal standing is high and that breeds ever more confidence. In a general sense you can forge ahead but the best area of life at this time is definitely going to be associated with personal and romantic matters. The words of love you utter today are imbued with sincerity and a poetic appeal others can't ignore.

30 THURSDAY *Moon Age Day 26 Moon Sign Taurus*

You may surprise others with the intensity of your views, especially at work. Some people might think that you tend towards superficiality but if that's what they think there's a good chance you will prove otherwise. Many of your thoughts run extremely deep at present and you won't be easily fooled by anyone.

July

2016

1 FRIDAY

Moon Age Day 27 Moon Sign Taurus

This may turn out to be an especially good time for problem solving. You have your clever head on today and can manage to fathom out all sorts of details that would normally prove to be very difficult. Not everyone is on your side now but the people who matter the most will be.

2 SATURDAY

Moon Age Day 28 Moon Sign Gemini

Domestic matters might seem to tie you down. It won't be long before you are back on top form but for the moment you will have to think carefully and discuss much. No matter how hard you try to get ahead right now it will probably seem as if something is holding you back.

3 SUNDAY

Moon Age Day 29 Moon Sign Gemini

Intimate relationships can be very rewarding today. You manage to say just the right things to please people and may also find that friends are especially warm and helpful. A few strangers may be difficult to deal with but that's a small price to pay on what should otherwise be an ideal day.

4 MONDAY

Moon Age Day 0 Moon Sign Cancer

There is important news coming your way, all you have to do to make use of it is to keep your eyes wide open. Confidence remains generally high and you shouldn't go short of fun. This is an ideal day for travel and for the sort of 'instant' meetings that could see you making a new friend.

5 TUESDAY *Moon Age Day 1 Moon Sign Cancer*

Take the time to address intensely personal issues at this time. People will take you every bit as seriously as you take yourself. Conversation comes easily, as is often the case for Aries, and you can be in just the right place to benefit materially when it matters the most. A day for having fun.

6 WEDNESDAY *Moon Age Day 2 Moon Sign Leo*

There is some subtle power play going on in your vicinity but these are games you may not be keen to join. Instead play a straight bat and make certain that everyone knows how you genuinely feel. When people have finished with the foolishness, you will be the one who is seen as trustworthy.

7 THURSDAY *Moon Age Day 3 Moon Sign Leo*

It's time to focus squarely on projects to be done at work or at home. A day of activity is on the cards and one that offers a variety of different possibilities. What you choose to do with them in an exact sense is clearly up to you at this time. Don't be afraid to mix business and pleasure.

8 FRIDAY *Moon Age Day 4 Moon Sign Virgo*

Getting on with others at home can prove to be rather hard work today, which is why you might choose to get out and about if possible. Anytime this month would be good for taking a holiday, but the upcoming weekend might be the best time of all. A change of scene is what Aries now craves.

9 SATURDAY *Moon Age Day 5 Moon Sign Virgo*

It is now a good time to capitalise on any new opportunity that comes along. Do what you can to get specific jobs out of the way, particularly if you have been making changes at home. Socially you need the cut and thrust of as many different sorts of personalities as you can possibly manage.

10 SUNDAY *Moon Age Day 6 Moon Sign Virgo*

Your thirst for freedom and adventure is still marked. For days you have been straining at the leash and looking forward to as many new experiences as you could find. The coming week brings the chance to do something about those longings but probably not until after Tuesday.

11 MONDAY *Moon Age Day 7 Moon Sign Libra*

If you feel let down by a friend, maybe you should let them know it. You won't get very far beating about the bush. There are times when it is definitely sensible to bite your lip but this isn't one of them although, of course, it would be appropriate to make sure that you are diplomatic.

12 TUESDAY *Moon Age Day 8 Moon Sign Libra*

You may be in a less than dynamic mood at present. The 'lunar low' holds you back somewhat, but only in a limited sense bearing in mind other planetary trends. Your confidence may be dented by chance remarks, but bear in mind that this may only be because you take them out of context.

13 WEDNESDAY *Moon Age Day 9 Moon Sign Scorpio*

You now have the potential to express yourself more clearly than you have in recent days. Whether you are dealing with people you know well or even if you are contacting strangers, the things you say will make perfect sense and it is possible that you will make some professional progress.

14 THURSDAY *Moon Age Day 10 Moon Sign Scorpio*

Mentally uplifting experiences are now coming in thick and fast. Today is likely to offer much more in the way of excitement than has been around for quite a while. Get any necessary chores out of the way early in the day and leave time later to simply enjoy yourself, probably in the company of exciting people.

15 FRIDAY *Moon Age Day 11 Moon Sign Scorpio*

This is likely to be one of your better days when it comes to making plans and for travel of any sort. This part of July would be an excellent time for a holiday. You would have the chance to recharge your batteries, whilst retaining enough energy to have some real fun on the way.

16 SATURDAY *Moon Age Day 12 Moon Sign Sagittarius*

Emotional issues could prove to be somewhat demanding at the moment and you may decide to shelve them for a while. It might be best to keep yourself busy in other ways. Certainly there is no shortage of things to be done if you are at work and it is possible that you will be quite busy on the social front.

17 SUNDAY *Moon Age Day 13 Moon Sign Sagittarius*

You could have a tendency to overlook small but essential details today. It is very important to concentrate on the matter in hand, even though there may be many considerations clouding your mind. Keep abreast of news and current events because later in the day this sort of knowledge will prove essential.

18 MONDAY *Moon Age Day 14 Moon Sign Capricorn*

Personal effectiveness and your influence over others could seem somewhat limited. That is one of the reasons why you need to be taking life at face value and not expecting too much of yourself or those around you. If you relax, the day ought to pass well enough and may even bring some unexpected events.

19 TUESDAY *Moon Age Day 15 Moon Sign Capricorn*

Analysing your true inner feelings today should allow you to express both your ideas and emotions thoroughly and meaningfully at this time. You are certainly likely to be working hard now and won't brook a great deal of interference in any situation that has a bearing on your professional future.

20 WEDNESDAY *Moon Age Day 16 Moon Sign Capricorn*

Your personal relationships need an extra boost and this can only really come from your direction. Be willing to pay a few compliments and don't leave people in the dark when it comes to arrangements that directly affect their lives. There isn't room for the overbearing type of Aries right now.

21 THURSDAY *Moon Age Day 17 Moon Sign Aquarius*

Life in general will prove to be far more hectic than you might have imagined. Things are getting more interesting and the dynamic side of Aries is once again on display. It hasn't always been easy to get your message across in recent days but that is a state of affairs that now changes rapidly.

22 FRIDAY *Moon Age Day 18 Moon Sign Aquarius*

Look out for an important phase of self-determination, which started yesterday and continues unabated at this time. Get financial details sorted out today and be willing to do whatever it takes to get the details of your life into shape. Conforming to the expectations of those around you may not be easy.

23 SATURDAY *Moon Age Day 19 Moon Sign Pisces*

Your powers of attraction are not in short supply. Even in relationships which have nothing at all to do with romance you make the best of impressions. Getting along with others should prove to be easier than has been the case for a number of days and this especially relates to superiors or those who have influence.

24 SUNDAY *Moon Age Day 20 Moon Sign Pisces*

Although arguments can crop up in personal relationships, you should not allow these to mar the day in a general sense. The fact is that you are better off with lighter, less turgid relationships at present. Taking life too seriously might just take the edge off an otherwise eventful and quite stimulating sort of day.

25 MONDAY *Moon Age Day 21 Moon Sign Aries*

Your main assistant on the road to greater personal success right now is your own ability to see ahead of yourself. Social instincts are now strong again and you actively need the help and support of inspirational people. Go for all your goals with that naturally irresistible energy and large amounts of enthusiasm.

26 TUESDAY *Moon Age Day 22 Moon Sign Aries*

With energy now definitely at a peak you are in the most potentially successful time of the month. Be bold and brash because for the moment you can get away with it. Take the most important of your schemes and put them into practice. Socially speaking, life should be looking especially good.

27 WEDNESDAY *Moon Age Day 23 Moon Sign Taurus*

The green light is on for just about anything you care to undertake. With plenty of support from directions that really count, you can make the most of every passing moment. This part of the summer favours journeys, whether or not they are specifically geared towards pleasure.

28 THURSDAY *Moon Age Day 24 Moon Sign Taurus*

It could appear that others are making too much of issues you don't really consider to be important. Try to stretch your imagination however and to see things from their point of view. Socially speaking you should keep life as simple as you can, associating freely with just about anyone who comes along.

29 FRIDAY *Moon Age Day 25 Moon Sign Gemini*

Impressing others certainly isn't difficult now. You know where the best action is likely to be and, slowly but surely, you are recovering from some of the less fortunate astrological influences that have been surrounding you for a while. There are still matters that could be rather taxing but you manage to get through them.

30 SATURDAY *Moon Age Day 26 Moon Sign Gemini*

Though you find yourself involved in all sorts of arrangements this weekend, most of them are geared towards having fun, which ought to suit you down to the ground at this time. Routines could seem dull and you will be overthrowing convention at every turn. Personal choice is of the utmost importance to you now.

31 SUNDAY *Moon Age Day 27 Moon Sign Cancer*

It would be a good idea to put off major projects, at least for today. Somehow you will get most of what you want but you will either have to settle for second best, or else work that much harder for little gain. A better strategy would be to take a rest, whilst those around you take some of the strain.

August

2016

1 MONDAY *Moon Age Day 28 Moon Sign Cancer*

There probably isn't quite enough self-discipline around at present. The fact is that your love of freedom presently overcomes your determination to do things properly. It might be best to try to reach some sort of compromise if you are not to make mistakes now that will cause you problems later.

2 TUESDAY *Moon Age Day 0 Moon Sign Cancer*

Facing facts about yourself seems to be the thing at present. Today you may well turn your attention towards personal attachments and the way you are dealing with them. The constantly changing planetary scene brings a degree of humility and should allow you to show some self-sacrifice in your immediate relationships.

3 WEDNESDAY *Moon Age Day 1 Moon Sign Leo*

It's quite clear that you can't please all the people all the time today. As a result it would be rather futile to try. Allow certain individuals to go their own way, even if you know that there are going to be mistakes made. You gain more respect through judicious advice rather than by forcing your will on to others.

4 THURSDAY *Moon Age Day 2 Moon Sign Leo*

It will be clear that many people display goodwill in their dealings with you. Of course there have to be one or two exceptions. It's best not to dwell on these but rather to recognise and be grateful for the assistance that is on offer. The time is coming when travel begins to have a special appeal.

5 FRIDAY *Moon Age Day 3 Moon Sign Virgo*

Along comes the time when you would definitely welcome a total change of scene. The holiday period is at hand and even if you can only make short journeys today, the gains would be great. You genuinely want to have fun and tend to socialise easily with a whole host of different people.

6 SATURDAY *Moon Age Day 4 Moon Sign Virgo*

It is likely that you will be attracting the right sort of person into your life today – people who share your present sense of fun and who will do their best to keep you entertained. Social pleasures come your way and the desire to move about still predominates. Don't forget the needs of your partner or a loved one, though.

7 SUNDAY *Moon Age Day 5 Moon Sign Libra*

With the 'lunar low' comes the start of a short period that looks rather less appealing than the last few days may have seemed. In fact, once Monday is out of the way, you will be making good ground again. For the moment it would be best to go with the flow, particularly so when it comes to social events.

8 MONDAY *Moon Age Day 6 Moon Sign Libra*

This simply may not be your luckiest day this month. For this reason it would be best to stay away from any form of speculation and to keep yourself geared towards doing jobs that are strictly necessary. This won't prevent you from having fun, though your sense of humour might not be quite as well honed as usual right now.

9 TUESDAY *Moon Age Day 7 Moon Sign Libra*

This could easily prove to be one of the best days of the month when it comes to bringing a specific project to a successful conclusion. Not everyone is equally helpful, but those who are less so tend to be somewhat sidelined by you right now. Give yourself a pat on the back on account of a recent success.

10 WEDNESDAY *Moon Age Day 8 Moon Sign Scorpio*

Taking things very much in your stride now makes you one of the most popular people around. Even types who have found you difficult to deal with in the past will be making positive overtures in your direction at this stage. Deal with the practical requirements of life one at a time and don't allow yourself to be rushed.

11 THURSDAY *Moon Age Day 9 Moon Sign Scorpio*

Your powers of personality are strong and the determined face of Aries shows quite plainly. Not everyone takes kindly to the fact that 'you know best' and some sort of compromise will be required. This isn't easy to find within yourself because, in the main, your hunches turn out to be correct.

12 FRIDAY *Moon Age Day 10 Moon Sign Sagittarius*

Fresh initiatives are coming and along and if you are going to pay enough attention to them, one or two jobs already started will have to wait a while. Try to split your time between the practical realities of life and your own need to have fun. This is a special time of year and it will pass all too quickly, so use it wisely.

13 SATURDAY *Moon Age Day 11 Moon Sign Sagittarius*

There is plenty to keep you on the go this weekend. It's true that not all of it proves to be that interesting, though you should still be able to derive a good deal of pleasure from life. In particular you can take warmth from the actions and reactions of loved ones, which seem custom-made to make you feel happy.

14 SUNDAY *Moon Age Day 12 Moon Sign Sagittarius*

Getting things working on a practical level is not without its problems right now. In order to do something specific you might have to jettison one or two of your hopes in other directions. This is called compromise and is something you understand only too well as a rule. At the moment trends make it more difficult than usual.

15 MONDAY *Moon Age Day 13 Moon Sign Capricorn*

Stay busy and active today and you will make the most of what is on offer. Sociable and especially willing to do what you can for the world at large, you should also notice that your popularity is well accented at this time. Slight changes in your lifestyle are also in the offing.

16 TUESDAY *Moon Age Day 14 Moon Sign Capricorn*

Don't allow anyone to interfere with your personal freedom today. People may not intend to tread on your toes but that's the way it is likely to seem. As far as travel is concerned, the further you roam, the better you are likely to feel. Excellent opportunities may come from seeking fresh fields and pastures new.

17 WEDNESDAY *Moon Age Day 15 Moon Sign Aquarius*

There is no need to rush at the moment. Most jobs, especially those in and around your home, will become far more enjoyable if you simply take your time. What is needed in your life today is a great sense of balance. For once you should discover that you don't really need the company of others.

18 THURSDAY *Moon Age Day 16 Moon Sign Aquarius*

If you find yourself involved in a strong disagreement with someone, particularly regarding a work issue, you will gain most by standing back. Confrontation really doesn't help at this time and only serves to entrench attitudes. In any argument at present you should show how flexible and fair you can be.

19 FRIDAY *Moon Age Day 17 Moon Sign Pisces*

Positive planetary highlights are in place, though you may be deliberately slowing things down. The more sensitive qualities within you have also been given a boost and this is an ideal time to speak words of love. Family members make positive overtures to you and bring new and fresh incentives into your life.

20 SATURDAY *Moon Age Day 18 Moon Sign Pisces*

Time spent alone today won't be at all wasted. You need to rest a little, ahead of a still more positive phase that lies only a day away. Any sort of job that requires that extra amount of patience should be addressed at the moment. There is help available when you are out of your depth personally.

21 SUNDAY *Moon Age Day 19 Moon Sign Aries*

An excellent Sunday is forecast by the arrival of the 'lunar high'. Times have been generally good for the last two weeks and now you can put all your recent success into one basket and make it work even better for you. Aries is certainly no shrinking violet during this part of the month.

22 MONDAY *Moon Age Day 20 Moon Sign Aries*

The 'lunar high' continues and brings better general luck. It's time to chance your arm somewhat, even if that only means daring to go on that fairground ride you have avoided before. There's a holiday spirit in your heart, whether or not you are actually free to pursue it directly at the moment.

23 TUESDAY *Moon Age Day 21 Moon Sign Taurus*

Don't be afraid to make a snap decision if that's what it takes to get things moving. There are some fairly slow and steady types around just now and that doesn't suit you particularly well. Certainly you have to be patient, because not everyone is like you. All the same a gentle nudge will help people far beyond your own life.

24 WEDNESDAY *Moon Age Day 22 Moon Sign Taurus*

Just when you appear to be on top form a few constraints come along. Not everyone you deal with is likely to agree with your point of view. Since you don't relish being crossed at the moment you might react strongly. Actually it would be much better to allow those around you to follow their own chosen path, at least for now.

25 THURSDAY *Moon Age Day 23 Moon Sign Gemini*

There is little doubt that you are quite willing today to roll up your sleeves and get stuck into matters that have been awaiting your attention for a while. There are expansive possibilities professionally and you have a willingness to co-operate that could see you getting on better in some ways than you might have expected.

26 FRIDAY *Moon Age Day 24 Moon Sign Gemini*

Avoid allowing yourself to become side tracked when what is really needed is hard and sustained effort. Concentrating on one job at once is important for the moment. By the time the working day is out of the way you should be in a good frame of mind to relax – that is if you haven't forgotten what that means!

27 SATURDAY *Moon Age Day 25 Moon Sign Gemini*

Expect general trends to be working in your favour, though there is an inevitable slowing for today and tomorrow. You might not take too kindly to this fact, though it may be that you have been burning the candle at both ends for so many days now you will react positively to any sort of steadier pace.

28 SUNDAY *Moon Age Day 26 Moon Sign Cancer*

You should find that it takes very little effort to make the very best impression on the world at large. This is likely to have been a generally excellent week in terms of friendship and association and today is no exception. It's likely that you will be planning for an interesting day and all you have to do now is to follow through.

29 MONDAY *Moon Age Day 27 Moon Sign Cancer*

Social and co-operative matters should put you at the forefront of life today. The weekend offered you the chance to be rather more circumspect and it is as a result of this that you operate even better at the start of this week. Romance is likely for many Aries subjects, even some who are not expecting it.

30 TUESDAY *Moon Age Day 28 Moon Sign Leo*

As far as work is concerned the astrological trends remain generally positive. Don't spend too much time looking at what you have to do. It would be better by far to simply pitch in and show your mettle. When you need support you can find it, sometimes from a fairly surprising direction.

31 WEDNESDAY ☿ *Moon Age Day 29 Moon Sign Leo*

Your ego is still strong and that's what gets you through one or two slightly contentious issues. This doesn't mean to say that you choose to argue. Rather the reverse is true since you are able to see alternative points of view and to cope with them. Genuine warmth shows in your personal attachments.

1 THURSDAY ☿ *Moon Age Day 0 Moon Sign Virgo*

The first day of September could turn out to be somewhat stressful. Maybe you haven't dealt with jobs that deserved your attention previously, in which case you will have to put in that extra bit of effort now. Enlist the support of interested friends and be willing to take on board the needs of others.

2 FRIDAY ☿ *Moon Age Day 1 Moon Sign Virgo*

All that is happening around you in a professional sense should appear to be extremely rewarding right now. Confidence remains generally high and you can afford to take the odd risk, even with people who might have been somewhat awkward in the past. Your creative potential is good at the moment.

3 SATURDAY ☿ *Moon Age Day 2 Moon Sign Virgo*

Life continues at a fairly swift pace and offers incentives at every turn. You are behaving as a true Aries should and soaking up the social possibilities with very little trouble. In truth, your constancy in personal attachments might not be all that others would wish but socially speaking you feel the need to spread yourself around.

4 SUNDAY ☿ *Moon Age Day 3 Moon Sign Libra*

Don't expect too much of yourself today. Take the time to realise where many of the benefits in your life come from. This is an ideal day to look at situations relating to relatives and friends. You are fairly selfless at present and have much to offer people who are far less dynamic than you are.

5 MONDAY ☿ *Moon Age Day 4 Moon Sign Libra*

You may find power somewhat hard to find right now. The 'lunar low' should not throw a spanner in the works where your ongoing efforts are concerned but it certainly can slow some of them down a little. Creating a comfortable space for yourself might appeal and you really should spend time pleasing yourself.

6 TUESDAY ☿ *Moon Age Day 5 Moon Sign Scorpio*

Although today may be a relaxed day as far as your personal life is concerned, this probably won't be the case in practical matters. Be prepared for everyone to demand your attention at the same time, leaving you dealing with a dozen jobs and probably getting none of them done adequately. Tomorrow may be better!

7 WEDNESDAY ☿ *Moon Age Day 6 Moon Sign Scorpio*

Professional success at the moment tends to be very much a case of who you know. Cultivating the right sort of associations is therefore very important. Concern for loved ones appears to be abating now and probably won't be an issue throughout most of today. Friends may be a different kettle of fish altogether.

8 THURSDAY ☿ *Moon Age Day 7 Moon Sign Scorpio*

You might find yourself wishing today that things could move faster than they appear to be doing at this time. If so you need to work a bit harder to bring changes about. A little confidence goes a long way, but works best when you know what you are talking about. Maybe some research would do the trick?

9 FRIDAY ☿ *Moon Age Day 8 Moon Sign Sagittarius*

It's time for some light relief, even though you may be almost entirely committed to your working life today. The practical joker within you is on display but nobody really minds this since Aries is looking for fun. Most important of all you can help others to have a really good day.

10 SATURDAY ☿ *Moon Age Day 9 Moon Sign Sagittarius*

Along comes a socially enjoyable period, thanks to the present position of the Moon. This weekend should have much going for it romantically, that is if you are on the lookout for love. Travel might once again become an issue, maybe in the company of people you both like and respect.

11 SUNDAY ☿ *Moon Age Day 10 Moon Sign Capricorn*

Try to avoid small but needless accidents today by paying attention to whatever you are doing. Mars is not doing you any favours at the moment and its position can lead to carelessness. On a much better note you will have the chance to show the really romantic side of your nature before very long.

12 MONDAY ☿ *Moon Age Day 11 Moon Sign Capricorn*

Contact with people you know well can lead to some interesting possibilities. At home you are creative and anxious to brighten up your surroundings in some way. In any situation that leaves you feeling as though life has been second-rate recently, you need to put in that extra bit of effort.

13 TUESDAY ☿ *Moon Age Day 12 Moon Sign Aquarius*

This may be a good time to assess the progress you have been making in your life generally. Although a busy sort of day, there are moments to think again about specific events and to put right those situations that didn't turn out quite the way you may have expected. Try to remain optimistic.

14 WEDNESDAY ☿ *Moon Age Day 13 Moon Sign Aquarius*

Impatience with specific obligations is part of the package you have to deal with today. You would much rather be giving your time to grandiose new schemes and maybe to some ventures that others would describe as odd or even foolish. Follow your own ideas if you are sure of them.

15 THURSDAY ☿ *Moon Age Day 14 Moon Sign Aquarius*

A specific domestic matter could prove to be irritating, or in a rare case, downright annoying. It won't help to lose your cool, so show yourself and the world that you can come out of the other side with your temper intact. It's true that some people can be really stupid but nobody is perfect, not even Aries.

16 FRIDAY ☿ *Moon Age Day 15 Moon Sign Pisces*

You may see some material gains coming your way at any time now. Keep your eye on the ball when it comes to new projects and put in that extra bit of effort that makes all the difference in the end. Recent successes only add incentive to your determination to go even further as the days pass.

17 SATURDAY ☿ *Moon Age Day 16 Moon Sign Pisces*

Ingenuity is the name of the game today. Whatever you do has a certain 'edge' to it and it is once again easy to impress those around you, some of whom have the ability to make your life easier later on. Confidence is not lacking and you should be willing to take that extra chance that could bring you success.

18 SUNDAY ☿ *Moon Age Day 17 Moon Sign Aries*

The Moon returns to your zodiac sign, offering a fascinating if somewhat hectic time. Although you may have to act very much on impulse your instincts are well tuned at present and you should not have too much difficulty getting your message across to anyone at all. Lady Luck ought to be on your side now.

19 MONDAY ☿ *Moon Age Day 18 Moon Sign Aries*

Good fortune follows you around like a friend right now, offering you the chance to get ahead in ways you hadn't expected. People will gather round to lend a hand and should create an interesting set of circumstances for you. Your kindness is clearly on display at this time.

20 TUESDAY ☿ *Moon Age Day 19 Moon Sign Taurus*

There may be a tendency for you to run out of steam all too quickly today and so it would be sensible not to take on more than you have to, at least early in the day. By the afternoon you should be back into your stride, with an evening that could easily be dedicated to having fun.

21 WEDNESDAY ☿ *Moon Age Day 20 Moon Sign Taurus*

Though you seem to be on a winning streak today when it comes to material considerations, not everyone seems to have you at the top of their popularity list. There isn't too much you can do about this situation, except to be patient and to understand you can't please all of the people all of the time.

22 THURSDAY *Moon Age Day 21 Moon Sign Gemini*

Minor mishaps in your daily life mean that you must exercise a little more care in a general sense. Although not a dangerous day, you may be clumsy and end up having to do some jobs time and again. Get yourself into the swing of requirements at work and listen to what superiors have to say about your recent efforts.

23 FRIDAY *Moon Age Day 22 Moon Sign Gemini*

Money comes your way from a whole host of different possible directions. You shouldn't expect to win the lottery tonight because cash arrives in smaller and more regular amounts for most Aries people right now. All the same, good luck is on your side, so it might be worth a small, considered flutter.

24 SATURDAY *Moon Age Day 23 Moon Sign Cancer*

Your financial powers should remain in the ascendant this weekend, so that is one sphere of life that you won't be worrying about too much. Socially speaking you will be in the market for a good time and making the best of any opportunity for diversion that is offered to you by well-meaning relatives and friends.

25 SUNDAY *Moon Age Day 24 Moon Sign Cancer*

Socially speaking you now find yourself going through a somewhat more reluctant phase. Although there is a good deal of encouragement coming from a number of different sources you will be happy to retreat into yourself, not a normal state of affairs for anyone born under the zodiac sign of Aries.

26 MONDAY *Moon Age Day 25 Moon Sign Leo*

Your practical skills today are considerable and you should discover a number of unfinished plans that now take on a new lease of life as far as your life generally is concerned. Don't be shy to tell others how you feel, particularly when it comes to emotional responses and certain situations that don't please you.

27 TUESDAY *Moon Age Day 26 Moon Sign Leo*

You can speed ahead now with just about any sort of project that really takes your fancy. Working Aries people should capitalise on the current good trends created by position of the Moon, which brings greater commitment and a determination to overturn obstacles. Find some time to tell loved ones how important they are to you.

28 WEDNESDAY *Moon Age Day 27 Moon Sign Virgo*

Seek out mental pursuits and get on with them as soon as you can. These should include co-operative ventures and bring you into contact with some very interesting individuals. You might even find yourself rubbing shoulders with the famous, or those who excel in some sort of sporting activity.

29 THURSDAY *Moon Age Day 28 Moon Sign Virgo*

If ever there was a part of the month when it proved possible to please all of the people for at least most of the time, this is it. Whatever you want from life is worth a shot, especially when you need other people on board to assist you. Confronting issues from the past probably isn't a good idea however.

30 FRIDAY *Moon Age Day 0 Moon Sign Virgo*

General trends now assist in making relationships ever more contented, at least from your perspective. Nevertheless it might be worth asking a few leading questions since there are likely to be at least a few people around who don't entirely hold your present point of view. Be patient with younger family members.

2016

1 SATURDAY *Moon Age Day 1 Moon Sign Libra*

Certain expectations will probably have to be played down today. Although the 'lunar low' doesn't have too much of a bearing on your life you could be feeling as though things are not turning out entirely as you would wish. Take advantage of good social possibilities towards the end of the day

2 SUNDAY *Moon Age Day 2 Moon Sign Libra*

Although there is little in the way of self-discipline about at this time, perhaps you should tell yourself that this is, after all, a Sunday. You are entitled to some time away from responsibility and should not get irritated with yourself simply because you do not feel like putting yourself out for purely practical reasons.

3 MONDAY *Moon Age Day 3 Moon Sign Scorpio*

There may be certain issues to bear in mind when you are dealing with others today and a sympathetic attitude would clearly work best. It is possible that in one way or another you could be feeling put upon, though in reality all you need to do is to talk things through to find even usually difficult people easy to handle.

4 TUESDAY *Moon Age Day 4 Moon Sign Scorpio*

This is one of the best days of the month for being in social situations and for getting on well with people generally. Some of the more critical types who were around earlier in the month are now less in evidence. Make the most of outings or the chance to meet new people on a one-to-one basis.

5 WEDNESDAY *Moon Age Day 5 Moon Sign Scorpio*

It is possible that for the first time in many days you will find at least some people unresponsive and difficult to deal with. This is a sign that you need to concentrate your efforts more specifically. Routines could get on your nerves for a few days but it will still be necessary to sort out some important details.

6 THURSDAY *Moon Age Day 6 Moon Sign Sagittarius*

Along comes a phase that definitely does benefit personal relationships. You should discover now that things do go better in pairs and that you have all you need to get your own way. What won't help is that Aries tendency to dominate either people or situations. An easy-going attitude definitely works best today.

7 FRIDAY *Moon Age Day 7 Moon Sign Sagittarius*

A long-standing commitment needs extra thinking about right now. Rules and regulations should be easier than usual to deal with, perhaps because you tend to make them up for yourself as you go along today. Your means of communication is good and some better luck may show itself later in the day.

8 SATURDAY *Moon Age Day 8 Moon Sign Capricorn*

Today marks the start of a transitional period during which many factors in your life will have to be looked at in a new and perhaps a very different way. A little physical discomfort of some sort almost certainly won't last long, though this may not be the best time for embarking on some new keep fit routine.

9 SUNDAY *Moon Age Day 9 Moon Sign Capricorn*

The social world, though quite clearly busy, may have less to offer you than has been the case for the last week or so. This shouldn't worry you too much. On the contrary you now turn your attention towards more practical issues and can be fairly ruthless when dealing with matters you know to be of supreme importance.

10 MONDAY *Moon Age Day 10 Moon Sign Capricorn*

There is a strong tendency at the start of this week for you to cast your mind backward, towards specific aspects of the past. Whether or not there is any practical gain to be had from this pursuit remains to be seen. What is clear is that you need to keep at least one eye on the future too.

11 TUESDAY *Moon Age Day 11 Moon Sign Aquarius*

No matter how you choose to express yourself at the moment there is a definite chance that you will run into some problems. It might be suggested that the best way round this sort of dilemma is to keep your mouth shut altogether, at least for now. These trends don't really have a bearing on personal attachments.

12 WEDNESDAY *Moon Age Day 12 Moon Sign Aquarius*

Your main concern right now is to improve your life in just about any way you find to be possible. The way forward is towards a greater degree of simplicity and to spend time with tasks that don't demand too much of you. Alterations to the periphery of life can have a great bearing further down the line, too.

13 THURSDAY *Moon Age Day 13 Moon Sign Pisces*

Look out for an 'off with the old and on with the new' sort of attitude which develops around now. Whatever is not working well in your life should probably be abandoned, in favour of alterations that bring you more in line with the way things should be. Personal attachments remain untouched by these trends.

14 FRIDAY *Moon Age Day 14 Moon Sign Pisces*

It may be that trying to please too many people today is something of a mistake. Better by far to concentrate your efforts on those you know well. Avoid saying 'yes' simply for the sake of popularity, since this is only likely to bring you some problems further down the line, when you will have to be honest.

15 SATURDAY *Moon Age Day 15 Moon Sign Aries*

The Moon moves into your sign and should bring with it a number of opportunities that look especially good. This is not a time when you will want to spend hours sorting out details. Once you have made up your mind to a specific course of action, get stuck in and show the world what you are made of.

16 SUNDAY *Moon Age Day 16 Moon Sign Aries*

This is almost certainly not a day to be too careful. The odd gamble can pay off well, as long as you make sure that you do not ignore your intuition, which works well right now. Financial objectives in particular are dealt with easily but you have an especially good ability to get on with those around you.

17 MONDAY *Moon Age Day 17 Moon Sign Taurus*

All aspects of communication are a gas at this time. With some entertaining people on the horizon and almost everything going your way, the time has come to put your thoughts into tangible form. Almost anyone will be pleased to hear what you have to say and their reactions could be surprising.

18 TUESDAY *Moon Age Day 18 Moon Sign Taurus*

You will now be at your most contented when you are on the move. Try to avoid staying too long in one place and keep your interests light and perhaps even superficial. What you definitely don't want at present is to be bogged down by circumstances and situations that you find boring.

19 WEDNESDAY *Moon Age Day 19 Moon Sign Gemini*

Your daily life is likely to be busier than ever, with material considerations taking the centre stage position. Get a few jobs out of the way today, even though they are not strictly necessary at this time. Later in the week your schedule is likely to be very rushed and you will need all the spare moments you can find.

20 THURSDAY *Moon Age Day 20 Moon Sign Gemini*

Where social matters are concerned you seem to be on top form. Mixing and mingling with a whole host of different types, you have the bit between your teeth when it comes to organising events and get-togethers. Romance is close for some Aries types, especially the young or young-at-heart.

21 FRIDAY *Moon Age Day 21 Moon Sign Cancer*

Most fulfilment today will come from private and domestic matters. It won't be possible for you to remove yourself from the real world altogether, but that is what you may feel like doing at times. This sort of Aries is rarely seen and your general attitude could prove to be quite a mystery to some.

22 SATURDAY *Moon Age Day 22 Moon Sign Cancer*

The emphasis is on material security and you are still unlikely to be biting off as much as you often do. Now you are steadier in your thought processes and more willing to see tasks through to their logical end. Socially speaking you are happy and sunny – in fact the perfect Aries as far as most people are concerned.

23 SUNDAY *Moon Age Day 23 Moon Sign Leo*

A high profile can be all-important today. The Moon is in Leo and so is angled well to your Sun sign. Other planetary indications assure you of a greater degree of popularity and an ability to get on side with people who might not have given you reason to believe they were particularly keen on you before.

24 MONDAY *Moon Age Day 24 Moon Sign Leo*

Your most meaningful moments today are with family members and friends who have been a part of your life for a long time. This would be a good day for domestic shopping or for making some sort of change around the house; possibly one that is geared towards your comfort in the winter months ahead.

25 TUESDAY *Moon Age Day 25 Moon Sign Leo*

Your social popularity is still very high. Splitting your time between friends and those at home is something you will have to try hard to achieve right now. It isn't always going to be easy but then taking the simple path in life isn't of that much interest to the average Aries individual.

26 WEDNESDAY *Moon Age Day 26 Moon Sign Virgo*

If you find yourself at loggerheads regarding a joint financial matter it would be best to stand back and try to look at things from a totally impartial point of view. Avoid getting tied up in red tape because your natural reaction at the moment would be to push your way through it. That could make you some enemies.

27 THURSDAY *Moon Age Day 27 Moon Sign Virgo*

You now tend to back down in discussions at home, whilst out there in the wider world you stick up for yourself totally. If you work with someone you love the result might be rather confusing. This duality of nature is not typical of your zodiac sign at all, so thank goodness it is a very temporary phenomenon.

28 FRIDAY *Moon Age Day 28 Moon Sign Libra*

This is generally a good time to play life steadily and not to attempt any major coup, particularly in a business sense. Once you have decided on a particular course of action you might have to wait until after the weekend to put it into action. In extreme cases it will be a few days before you can make genuine progress.

29 SATURDAY *Moon Age Day 29 Moon Sign Libra*

If there are genuine setbacks now on the road to success, the best way forward is to simply wait and see. With the weekend here it is possible that you have already written off today in terms of practical gains, leaving the field free for personal enjoyment, which is not hindered by present trends.

30 SUNDAY *Moon Age Day 0 Moon Sign Libra*

Talks with others could prove enlightening during this weekend period. This is likely to be especially true if you are at work, with the possibility of promotion coming along for some Aries people at this time. Keep your most entertaining side hidden until the evening though because there are happy times on offer.

31 MONDAY *Moon Age Day 1 Moon Sign Scorpio*

You may feel that getting through to others is not half as easy as you would wish today. This said, some of the problems could actually be caused by those other people. The Aries ego isn't burning quite as brightly as usual at present, but don't allow this trend to make you feel that problems are always your fault.

♈

November

2016

1 TUESDAY *Moon Age Day 2 Moon Sign Scorpio*

It could be that for some Aries subjects there are slight difficulties surrounding an intimate relationship. Getting this sorted out will be your number one priority. Meanwhile you are also busy in a practical sense and more than willing to share some of your present professional knowledge with others.

2 WEDNESDAY *Moon Age Day 3 Moon Sign Sagittarius*

Your idealism is very strong and there isn't much doubt about your determination to follow specific routes, once you have made up your mind. This could make you appear somewhat less than flexible when seen through the eyes of others, a state of affairs that may not help you too much in the short-term.

3 THURSDAY *Moon Age Day 4 Moon Sign Sagittarius*

If there is any uncertainty in your life today it can probably be best addressed by turning to someone who is a professional in their own specific field. There are always individuals around who will do everything they can to help you. This is especially true in light of your own willingness to help others.

4 FRIDAY *Moon Age Day 5 Moon Sign Sagittarius*

Any chance to strike up some form of new social contract should be grasped with both hands. This is most certainly the case when you are dealing with unconventional types, many of whom seem to be especially attractive to you at this time. Have fun when you are away from work and socialise as much as possible.

5 SATURDAY *Moon Age Day 6 Moon Sign Capricorn*

The real enjoyment that comes into your life is inclined to do so in and around your home. This has been the tendency for some time now and remains the case across the weekend. You can rely on relatives to do you favours. More importantly, intimate contacts are offering so much more than usual.

6 SUNDAY *Moon Age Day 7 Moon Sign Capricorn*

The green light is on regarding general progress and you know what you want from life at this time. The true nature of Aries is now beginning to show, offering incentives that have been absent for some time. Grab life with both hands and enjoy the advantages that are now on offer.

7 MONDAY *Moon Age Day 8 Moon Sign Aquarius*

A light-hearted approach to all matters of love and romance now comes along. With a smile on your face for most of the day you can be an inspiration to others and keep everyone more or less happy. This is the side of Aries that the world really adores and most of the people you meet will share your attitude.

8 TUESDAY *Moon Age Day 9 Moon Sign Aquarius*

Although you are speaking and acting well at present, it is just possible that some misunderstandings at home could prove to be a problem. You need to find moments to explain yourself fully, even when you are so busy in other ways. Trying to fit in everything you want to do right now won't be easy.

9 WEDNESDAY *Moon Age Day 10 Moon Sign Pisces*

Social issues have rather less going for them today, which is why it would be sensible to turn your attention towards practicalities instead. At work you are progressive and even dynamic. It won't be long before it seems that the whole world is turning to you for specific advice of the sort that Aries now finds easy to dispense.

10 THURSDAY *Moon Age Day 11 Moon Sign Pisces*

A series of pleasurable diversions, away from strictly practical day-to-day issues, are more than likely at this time. Give yourself over fully to having fun when the chance arises and don't be bogged down with details that don't really matter. Creative potential is good, especially in and around your home.

11 FRIDAY *Moon Age Day 12 Moon Sign Pisces*

Your home life remains specifically rewarding, though that doesn't mean you are ignoring the more practical aspects of your life. What you manage today is a more than adequate balance, even if it does sometimes appear that you are burning the candle at both ends. Aries resilience is legendary and today you prove it.

12 SATURDAY *Moon Age Day 13 Moon Sign Aries*

With the 'lunar high' comes a definite sense of drive and enthusiasm. You shouldn't find it at all hard to ring the changes and you will be much more likely now to spend time away from home. Despite these facts, and the 'lunar high', you may feel happier if someone you know well is close at hand.

13 SUNDAY *Moon Age Day 14 Moon Sign Aries*

Pushing ahead and getting what you want from life are simply two of your talents right now. Energy is returning and you may look back at the last week or so, puzzled at the way you may have behaved. That doesn't matter. Simply strike while the iron is hot. Make gains and have fun, even though this is a Sunday.

14 MONDAY *Moon Age Day 15 Moon Sign Taurus*

There are ups and downs to deal with, and fortunately your ability to go to the heart of any specific matter is enhanced now. Gradually you see life as a more positive experience than might have been the case for a few days. Routines are not hard to address. Socially speaking, you may prefer the company of relatives.

15 TUESDAY *Moon Age Day 16 Moon Sign Taurus*

You need to be very aware of the motives of others at this time, particularly those who may have some sort of interest in fooling you in some way. Keep a high profile when you are in company and don't be put off by the sort of individual who naturally tends to be pessimistic. You can be a guiding force now.

16 WEDNESDAY *Moon Age Day 17 Moon Sign Gemini*

Don't let emotional issues dominate you today to the point that you forget about the practical matters of life. There are plenty of opportunities for you to make an extremely good impression and the sort of company around that you should find to be both stimulating and of use to you in terms of new ideas.

17 THURSDAY *Moon Age Day 18 Moon Sign Gemini*

There are changes taking place around you, whether or not you seem to be choosing them for yourself. In those situations where you have no power to alter the state of affairs it's best to go with the flow. Very few situations around you at present would work against your best interests.

18 FRIDAY *Moon Age Day 19 Moon Sign Cancer*

Today just could seem to be something of a comedown after recent events. Never mind, concentrate instead on the quieter aspects of the day and enjoy the relief of less activity. There should be plenty of people around who would be more than willing to share your leisure hours and who can lift your spirits no end.

19 SATURDAY *Moon Age Day 20 Moon Sign Cancer*

This continues to be a period of quiet mental stimulus and information. Stay tuned in to all that life is offering and don't allow others to bring you down. Someone you haven't seen for quite some time is likely to turn up again in your life at any time now and may bring some surprises with them.

20 SUNDAY *Moon Age Day 21 Moon Sign Leo*

Travel could now be subject to delays, probably through circumstances that are beyond your own control. Stay calm if things do go wrong, or else do what you can to redress the balance. Newer and better powers of communication are coming your way, thanks to changing planetary trends.

21 MONDAY *Moon Age Day 22 Moon Sign Leo*

You can clearly enjoy the best of both worlds today. On the one hand life can be romantic and emotionally rewarding, whilst on the other you have the ability to get practical jobs out of the way in no time at all. Your personality is entertaining and it is very easy for others to demonstrate how fond they are of you.

22 TUESDAY *Moon Age Day 23 Moon Sign Virgo*

Now is the moment to look at emotional issues in a dispassionate way and to sort them out as well and as quickly as you can. Certainly this should not be a long process because there are so many practical jobs around that also need your attention. Someone needs your timely advice, so keep your eyes open.

23 WEDNESDAY *Moon Age Day 24 Moon Sign Virgo*

Remove yourself from the company of those who seem determined to be losers. This really isn't your way and it can only depress you if you are constantly surrounded by moaners. Of course you will do what you can to help everyone but you are less willing to do so in the case of those who won't assist themselves.

24 THURSDAY *Moon Age Day 25 Moon Sign Libra*

Consider the present influences to be nothing more than a short layoff between more positive trends. Take time out to think about things and do your best to find enjoyment in low-key ways. Talking casually to people you really like is one way to avert your gaze from some of the apparent inadequacies around you.

25 FRIDAY *Moon Age Day 26 Moon Sign Libra*

Beware of potential setbacks. The 'lunar low' won't sap your resolve but it might prevent you from doing exactly what you would wish. In all probability you will find yourself being held back by circumstances beyond your own control. What cannot be altered must be endured. Once you realise this fact, you simply move on anyway.

26 SATURDAY *Moon Age Day 27 Moon Sign Libra*

A minor personal letdown from the friend is something you will simply have to accept. The trends generally are very good, even though the 'lunar low' is around for a day or two. This is the part of the month during which you are very good at thinking and planning, though less effective in a practical sense.

27 SUNDAY *Moon Age Day 28 Moon Sign Scorpio*

Be careful that you are not becoming obsessed in any way. This is particularly true when it comes to emotional ties and especially so for young or unattached Arians. It isn't easy to be objective at the moment but there ought to be plenty of advice on hand if you are willing to look for it.

28 MONDAY *Moon Age Day 29 Moon Sign Scorpio*

The situation regarding your career is somewhat complicated right now but there should be the promise of better things to come. Consider your options carefully and don't allow yourself to get drawn into discussions or arguments that have no purpose. Some discomfort can probably be expected from time to time today.

29 TUESDAY *Moon Age Day 0 Moon Sign Sagittarius*

The lighter side of life appears to be what you are seeking at present. Contribute to the general hilarity that surrounds you at this time, though since you are creating most of it that should not be difficult. Money pressures are likely to ease and you could even find yourself to be better off than you thought.

30 WEDNESDAY *Moon Age Day 1 Moon Sign Sagittarius*

Your profile is high at present and that means that attention is still coming your way, sometimes from less than favourable directions. Not all situations will be perfect but the majority need to suit you and there isn't much point in pretending otherwise. Simply stay away from those who don't interest you at all.

♈

December

2016

1 THURSDAY *Moon Age Day 2 Moon Sign Sagittarius*

The start of the month is likely to bring an emotional issue that will require some careful handling on your part. Avoid getting yourself into a state over things that can be sorted out easily if you keep your cool. Thoughts of Christmas will probably be on your mind already, though they should be positive ones.

2 FRIDAY *Moon Age Day 3 Moon Sign Capricorn*

You put a lot of energy into getting results and being generally busy. Of course this ensures that you get a great deal done but it will also cut down on the social time available. Exchange ideas, even with people you haven't altogether seen eye to eye with previously. By doing so you derive a new perspective.

3 SATURDAY *Moon Age Day 4 Moon Sign Capricorn*

Your ability to handle several different tasks at the same time is clearly marked today. This is Aries working at its best and so a happy time can be expected. Actually life may be a blur of activity on occasions, though it appears you should still find the time to spend with those who are dear to you.

4 SUNDAY *Moon Age Day 5 Moon Sign Aquarius*

Many issues can seem to be particularly fulfilling at the moment. Perhaps you now have a greater sense of financial security, or at the very least ideas that can bring it about. You are confident in your ability to do the right thing but be careful to side step the enquiries of a nosy friend.

5 MONDAY *Moon Age Day 6 Moon Sign Aquarius*

It could appear that friendly meetings and even business associations only have something going for them today when they are massaging your ego, which isn't small at present. That's part of your astrological nature, but you do have the ability to at least attempt humility from time to time.

6 TUESDAY *Moon Age Day 7 Moon Sign Aquarius*

It may be unwise to believe everything that you hear today. Although the majority of people are clearly doing what they can to tell you the truth, it may come down to being a matter of perspective at the end of the day. In other words nobody is deliberately trying to fool you, it simply seems that way.

7 WEDNESDAY *Moon Age Day 8 Moon Sign Pisces*

In terms of work your ability to get ahead may be subject to a number of small setbacks. Don't worry if this turns out to be the case because it's clear that you have your sights set on personal and social matters. Even Aries can't be all things to all people for every moment of each day.

8 THURSDAY *Moon Age Day 9 Moon Sign Pisces*

Your competitive side shows when you are involved in almost any sort of discussion. This would not be a good time to get too involved in sorting out the whole world however, since there is more than enough to do in your own life. Beware of spending too many hours simply proving other people wrong.

9 FRIDAY *Moon Age Day 10 Moon Sign Aries*

The 'lunar high' brings you to a physical and mental peak and the part of the month when you will really want to show what you are made of. The competitive edge begins to make itself felt and almost anything you do brings that Aries desire to win through, no matter what the opposition might be.

10 SATURDAY *Moon Age Day 11 Moon Sign Aries*

You could talk the hind leg off a donkey right now. That's good, because you also have the ability to get on with just about anyone. The genuinely likeable quality of your Aries nature is on display, which ensures popularity. In turn this gives you more confidence and closes a necessary circle of self-belief for you.

11 SUNDAY *Moon Age Day 12 Moon Sign Taurus*

Certain information is apt to go astray today, so it's important to watch what you are doing and to ask the right questions frequently. This state of affairs is down to short stay planetary influences so is a very fleeting phenomenon. Don't forget to support family members who are working hard now.

12 MONDAY *Moon Age Day 13 Moon Sign Taurus*

There isn't much doubt that some issues can be turned easily to your advantage. Seeking these out isn't as easy today as is going to prove to be the case tomorrow. A good deal of thought needs to go into planning your next move, particularly at work. You should also now be really looking ahead towards Christmas.

13 TUESDAY *Moon Age Day 14 Moon Sign Gemini*

The going is still very good when it comes to new incentives and alternative ways of looking at life. So capable are you today that it appears you have everything you need to mix business and pleasure in a totally successful sort of way. If you have been thinking about some new sort of regime, now is the time to get stuck in.

14 WEDNESDAY *Moon Age Day 15 Moon Sign Gemini*

A professional matter can go astray, leaving you floundering for an hour or two. If this turns out to be the case simply turn on all that practical Aries energy and pull yourself out of the problem. Socially speaking you are especially good company and should find your popularity extremely well accented now.

15 THURSDAY *Moon Age Day 16 Moon Sign Cancer*

This is an ideal period to try to broaden your horizons. Be careful what you take on though because Christmas is just around the corner and you don't want incentives to flag during the festive season. What might be best of all is to plan a strategy that commences almost at the start of the new year.

16 FRIDAY *Moon Age Day 17 Moon Sign Cancer*

It is one thing to be optimistic and quite another to believe that you can move mountains. What is called for now is a dose of realism, though allied to incentive and belief. If you can strike this happy medium there is almost nothing beyond your abilities. Romance seems to be knocking at any time now.

17 SATURDAY *Moon Age Day 18 Moon Sign Leo*

Pleasure pursuits and romantic issues are interesting you greatly at present. Some practical issues might also be coming to a head and you will want to do everything you can to encourage your own eventual success. That's fine but don't push too hard when life itself is in a position to help you out.

18 SUNDAY *Moon Age Day 19 Moon Sign Leo*

A strong sense of restlessness strikes home for some Aries subjects at present. This could be a reaction to the fact that social trends seem ruled by Christmas, something that probably won't suit you down to the ground. Look out for some sort of adventure and try to ring the changes in terms of social events.

19 MONDAY *Moon Age Day 20 Moon Sign Virgo*

This should prove to be a day for smooth professional progress, even if not everyone appears to be exactly on your side just for the moment. That's partly because you are more than willing to make a competition out of events that are not important at all. Don't defend yourself if you are not attacked.

20 TUESDAY ☿ *Moon Age Day 21 Moon Sign Virgo*

Some of you are going to be so busy on the social scene today that it becomes impossible to approach practical issues with quite the gusto you might wish. Never mind, what isn't sorted today can be dealt with later. In all probability you are so very active simply because Christmas is only a few days away.

21 WEDNESDAY ☿ *Moon Age Day 22 Moon Sign Virgo*

You should enjoy almost anything that life is throwing at you now. With a good sense of proportion, winning ways and a determination to end up at the front, you push on regardless. People love the fact that you don't give in, even on those rare occasions when the odds seem to be stacked against you.

22 THURSDAY ☿ *Moon Age Day 23 Moon Sign Libra*

Unfortunately some people are getting ahead faster than you are just now. There is little or nothing that you can do about this situation, at least not without wearing yourself out altogether. Why not show a greater willingness to let those around you do some of the work, whilst you take a backseat for once?

23 FRIDAY ☿ *Moon Age Day 24 Moon Sign Libra*

There are influences around today that can perk up your social and personal life no end, even though at the start of the day you will find the 'lunar low' still in operation. By lunchtime it isn't hard to find yourself working and playing hard again, and finally looking forward to what lies in store in the days ahead.

24 SATURDAY ☿ *Moon Age Day 25 Moon Sign Scorpio*

On a personal level you are feeling rather competitive. There's nothing at all new about that from an Aries perspective, though it's rather pointless proving your worth to people who recognise it well already. By the evening you should be more than willing to let your hair down and have some real fun.

25 SUNDAY ☿ *Moon Age Day 26 Moon Sign Scorpio*

A great Christmas Day is in the offing, even if you begin to run out of steam later in the day. Trends are variable and show you to be open-minded, well able to get on with a variety of different types and enjoying life to the full. Some of the surprises that come your way today should be especially delightful.

26 MONDAY ☿ *Moon Age Day 27 Moon Sign Scorpio*

Now you find yourself faced with another eventful and generally positive sort of day. With people constantly trying to gain your attention it could be somewhat difficult to please everyone, though you are certain to try. Family and friends are the ones who tend to win out as far as you are concerned now.

27 TUESDAY ☿ *Moon Age Day 28 Moon Sign Sagittarius*

Beware of a fairly up and down period where work is concerned, though of course if you are not at work this trend is hardly likely to have a bearing on your day. Certainly from a social point of view you look and feel good. Although you can't have quite everything you want romantically now, you won't fall far short.

28 WEDNESDAY ☿ *Moon Age Day 29 Moon Sign Sagittarius*

Though eager to get your ideas across, you will be rather too anxious to spread the word at this time. The fact is that you are likely to scare some people off, especially if you have to deal with types who are far less gregarious than you are. Slow and steady wins some sort of race that has social overtones.

29 THURSDAY ☿ *Moon Age Day 0 Moon Sign Capricorn*

Work matters are likely to keep you on the go at this time. If, on the other hand, you are away from work until after the new year, you are likely to be busy on the home front. Enjoying yourself can be tiring, which is why you need to turn your mind in more practical directions if possible.

30 FRIDAY ☿ *Moon Age Day 1 Moon Sign Capricorn*

For the first time since Christmas you could be quite happy to be away from the crowds for a few hours. Although there are things to do that make you appear quieter than usual, at least take some time out to let those around you know that you are not sulking about something. Extra effort with relatives is especially important.

31 SATURDAY ☿ *Moon Age Day 2 Moon Sign Capricorn*

The last day of the year offers you the chance to make a very positive social impact on the world at large. Aries is in the mood to party and there are people around who should be more than willing to join in. Don't take yourself or anyone else too seriously for the moment and concentrate on having fun.

RISING SIGNS FOR ARIES

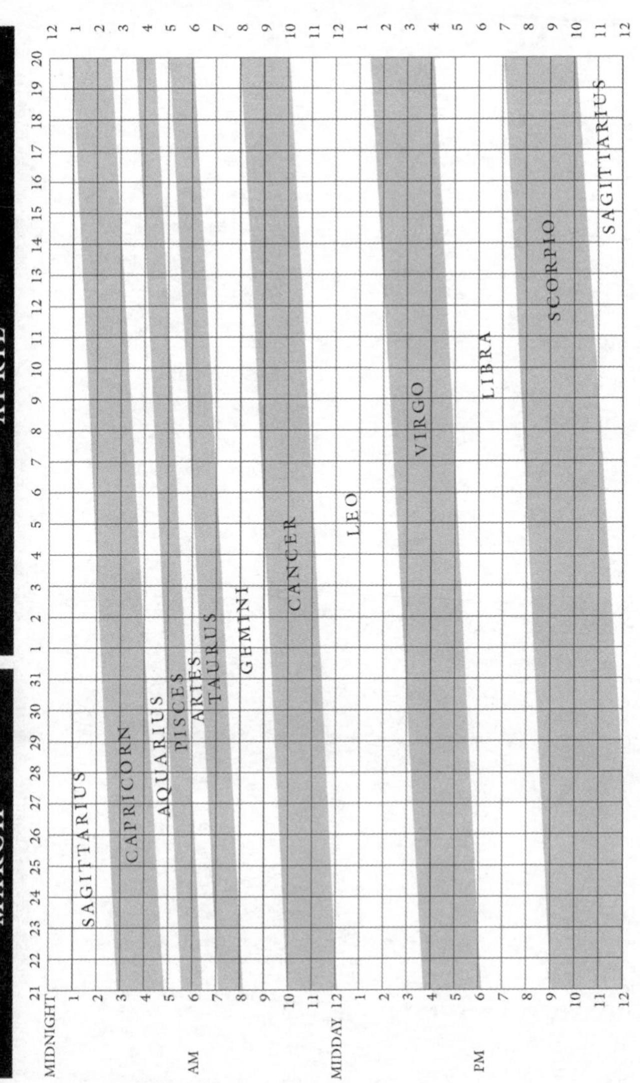

THE ZODIAC, PLANETS AND CORRESPONDENCES

The Earth revolves around the Sun once every calendar year, so when viewed from Earth the Sun appears in a different part of the sky as the year progresses. In astrology, these parts of the sky are divided into the signs of the zodiac and this means that the signs are organised in a circle. The circle begins with Aries and ends with Pisces.

Taking the zodiac sign as a starting point, astrologers then work with all the positions of planets, stars and many other factors to calculate horoscopes and birth charts and tell us what the stars have in store for us.

The table below shows the planets and Elements for each of the signs of the zodiac. Each sign belongs to one of the four Elements: Fire, Air, Earth or Water. Fire signs are creative and enthusiastic; Air signs are mentally active and thoughtful; Earth signs are constructive and practical; Water signs are emotional and have strong feelings.

It also shows the metals and gemstones associated with, or corresponding with, each sign. The correspondence is made when a metal or stone possesses properties that are held in common with a particular sign of the zodiac.

Finally, the table shows the opposite of each star sign – this is the opposite sign in the astrological circle.

Placed	Sign	Symbol	Element	Planet	Metal	Stone	Opposite
1	Aries	Ram	Fire	Mars	Iron	Bloodstone	Libra
2	Taurus	Bull	Earth	Venus	Copper	Sapphire	Scorpio
3	Gemini	Twins	Air	Mercury	Mercury	Tiger's Eye	Sagittarius
4	Cancer	Crab	Water	Moon	Silver	Pearl	Capricorn
5	Leo	Lion	Fire	Sun	Gold	Ruby	Aquarius
6	Virgo	Maiden	Earth	Mercury	Mercury	Sardonyx	Pisces
7	Libra	Scales	Air	Venus	Copper	Sapphire	Aries
8	Scorpio	Scorpion	Water	Pluto	Plutonium	Jasper	Taurus
9	Sagittarius	Archer	Fire	Jupiter	Tin	Topaz	Gemini
10	Capricorn	Goat	Earth	Saturn	Lead	Black Onyx	Cancer
11	Aquarius	Waterbearer	Air	Uranus	Uranium	Amethyst	Leo
12	Pisces	Fishes	Water	Neptune	Tin	Moonstone	Virgo